To Marilyn, With best wishes on the day of the "we will see" outcome!

Robert Worcester

1-7-2011

Sidetracked

A True-life Motoring Saga

Robert Maidment

To Tanya

P V H Books

First published in Great Britain in 2005
by P V H Books
Ann Suckling Road,
Little Wratting,
Suffolk CB9 7TA

Printed by Printwise (Haverhill) Ltd
Haverhill, Suffolk

Illustrations by Tony Jarmain

A Catalogueing-in-Publication record for this book is available from
the British Library.

ISBN 0-9550151-0-3

Contents

Chapter		Page

Acknowledgements

Telling the story of how and why a team of everyday people carried out a not-so-everyday project and the subsequent string of unlikely coincidences, I find myself in the debt of all too many. Firstly, there are the members of the team itself, especially those in and around the town of Haverhill, Suffolk. Without their expertise and tireless efforts, such an undertaking could never have been started, let alone finished and later 'happenings' would never have happened.

Next, I must thank my long-suffering right hand and fiercest critic Linda, my wife, without whose tireless support and editorial proofing, this book would never have passed its earliest stages. I must also especially thank Stuart Bladon and Norman Uhlir for their input, both technical and historical, to say nothing of the many other friends and acquaintances who, over the duration of the book's long compilation, have given invaluable and constructive advice whenever asked.

Then there are those who, against seemingly insurmountable odds, offered timely engineering contributions to the project itself: Colin Crabbe for his ongoing enthusiastic support; André Jute, for his excellent book, 'Designing and Building Special Cars' published by B. T. Batsford; Mithril Racing and MIRA for their generous uncharged-for evaluation of the finished product; and Matt & Michaline Larson and Ian Morton who gave so much of their time in so many ways.

I must also thank The Reverend Jim Faulconer of Kettering, Ohio for unearthing some hitherto unrealised family links and Maurice Hendry for his tireless efforts in helping uncover some long-forgotten fragments of motoring history. Then there was the RAC Club and the Beaulieu Motor Museum who helped unravel the mysteries surrounding a hundred-year-old motorcar.

Finally, my thanks must go to those at Courier Products during the earlier part of this story, whose loyal support added so much to the project's success as well as to the enjoyment of a most unlikely venture.

Foreword
by David Price

Take a number of enthusiastic and dedicated men, all motivated by the thought of developing a motorcar that could boast originality and excitement. Add to this a late-seventies luxury saloon to form the mechanical basis for an outrageous automotive project. What this provides is an extraordinary machine that is the very spirit of car development through the years. Rob's story with its many unexpected turns, both during and after construction, is not only informative – it is immense fun.

In the time that I was Chairman of Aston Martin Lagonda, I was able to indulge my love of the beautiful hand-built cars, with their flowing panels, their exotic upholstery and their engines that make such sweet music. Imagine my surprise – and delight – when I was first introduced to this product of love and dedication to detail. Anyone who has attempted to create the unusual, either professionally or privately, will be able to associate with many of the hurdles encountered in this book. Whether we have all cleared such hurdles as well – or at times as eccentrically or with such surprise results – as this team did, I must let you, the reader, decide.

Finally, the most important message comes in the later chapters: "It's a car – it needs to be used." However beautiful, however original, however expensive, a car is first and foremost there to be driven. I was therefore delighted to read of the daring feats that lead on to a motoring challenge, so obviously fraught with complications, and its ultimate success.

Finally, I wish all those involved every enjoyment and future success, and I have no doubt that this exotic Roadster will continue to bring much pleasure to enthusiasts and non-enthusiasts alike; this book will do the same.

David Price

Introduction

This story is intended as much for anyone who has ever contemplated creating something out of the ordinary, or who would just enjoy being a part of such an undertaking, as it is for all those who appreciate the joys of motoring, antique or otherwise. With this in mind, I have attempted to concentrate on the more interesting and entertaining aspects of what took place, while trying not to omit anything of interest to those with a more inquisitive or more technical nature.

To prevent confusion in the double meaning of certain words, there have had to be compromises in motoring terminology. These include: the lid on the front of a car – which generally hides the engine – being referred to as the bonnet, whereas the compartment at the back – which usually accommodates the luggage – is the trunk (the old-fashioned British term and present-day American). The wings are the visible pretty bits above the wheel openings as against the mudguards, which are seldom seen and do just that, namely guard against mud. And a roof, whether collapsible or otherwise, is always and only a roof.

I have tried throughout to retain the feeling of excitement and resolve, as well as the occasional note of maturity. That said, I hope the inclusion of earlier incidents, considered essential to the story as a whole, are both enjoyable and easy to relate to.

The sequence of events while undertaking the initial project, as well as a number of the earlier outings in the later chapters, are not necessarily in their true order and 'earlier days' are as best as I can remember. Yet, as unlikely as some aspects may seem, everything occurred as told.

Finally, any similarity between living persons and those referred to in the book, more likely than not is just that; and I sincerely hope that they, along with everyone else, enjoy the pages that follow.

1. Memories Aroused

Sir Stirling Moss arrived with a lady on each arm, neither of whom was Lady Moss. The great racing icon had come to lend his support to a once-in-a-lifetime endurance run of a young man and elderly machine. Miraculously, the challenge of completing a thousand miles in a hundred-year-old car over a mere nine days was still on course.

Two days earlier, local television had recorded the start, which had taken place fifty, ninety and a hundred years previously. Now, on the event's rest day, at a commemorative gathering in Crystal Palace Park, crowds had assembled in force. Apart from the trial itself, the prospect of meeting Sir Stirling Moss, and the possibility of his driving a few lucky people's cars, was to be the highlight of the day.

Earlier, alone in his wife's new Smart Car, Stirling had rounded a corner, found it not quite as he had anticipated and caught an inside wheel on the kerb, bursting a tyre. As he stood wondering what to do with a car that comes without a spare, two gallant ladies, fully intent on rescuing an elderly gentleman in distress, stopped to help. Realising on whom by chance they had stumbled, Stirling was scooped up and delivered to Crystal Palace post haste. There, with smiles of affection reserved solely for such enduring idols, the two ladies had kissed Stirling firmly on each cheek before departing with all-knowing waves of affection.

While willing volunteers headed off to rescue his car without a spare, Stirling engrossed himself in the day's festivities. Later, as he strolled with a small group in the warm autumn sunshine, making his way across the lawns between the imposing nineteenth-century Italian Terraces and a section of the old motor racing track, Stirling stopped beside the car that had been assigned as official Support Vehicle for the 1000-mile challenge.

"I like this one," he said, looking down the length of the shining thirties-style up-and-over bonnet and along the flowing wings fore and aft. Then, peering into its inviting interior: "What is it? It looks a bit special." Then, after a pause: "How does it drive?"

As the one primarily responsible for this sporting one-of-a-kind, I was summoned to explain. At first, I remained at a loss for words. The machine had already been the subject of a string of unlikely discoveries and incidents, including having been the trigger for re-enacting the present 1,000-mile challenge. Now, the world renowned racing driver was asking, "How does it drive?" Would he echo the views of others: "She handles well... has a good feel," as once observed by a long-time professional, rubber tearing from the tyres as we slid through a double corner on a high-speed track?

With continuing disbelief that Sir Stirling Moss should be taking a positive interest in our creation, I began to recollect, with equal disbelief, just how such a motorcar had first been conceived. I was quickly drawn back a decade and a half, back to an economic era of apparent unstoppable upward euphoria, in effect a time dominated by the belief that anything and everything was a good investment.

Extraordinary as it now seemed, while we stood discussing the result of one of those so deemed good investments, it had all begun one morning in the late nineteen-eighties with the arrival of an auctioneer's promotional postcard. Pictured on the front, posed alongside a grassy riverbank, was a glamorous nineteen-thirties Mercedes-Benz Roadster, top down and rearing to go. On the reverse were the details of its forthcoming sale.

"That's a fun looking machine," I had tentatively observed, as I extracted the card from the daily post.

"Yes, and it certainly has style," came the measured, almost jovial reply from over my shoulder.

Surprised by the positive reaction from someone who during our married life had normally cared little for such obscure objects, I studied the picture in more detail. With its graceful flowing lines, long protruding bonnet and tightly fitting cab, the elderly sports-car had to be the ultimate in motoring art. Yet, far from being cleaned and polished as might be expected for such an occasion, the once-proud machine appeared to have been found in the sea; or, at the very least, in the river beside which it now stood. Out of curiosity, I dialled the auctioneers.

"We've received the information on the Mercedes Roadster and wondered how much you were expecting for it," I enquired.

"We think she should reach about eight hundred thousand pounds sir," was the polite and immediate answer.

"Oh yes, I see, thank you," I replied, equally matter of factly while attempting to hide my astonishment, and said goodbye.

Was this some sort of madness? Was someone really going to pay the equivalent of half a dozen new Rolls-Royces for a jumble of metal and fabric that could probably be copied for a fraction of the cost? If so, I must have completely lost track of the classic car market in the excitement of an overheated economic boom.

"They think that wreck could sell for nearly a million pounds," I remarked, then jokingly added: "We can't afford it, we'll have to make one!"

"What a good idea," came the instant, and presumably intuitive retort – a remark that, although often regretted, has never been denied.

Taking the suggestion rather more literally than intended, I began to wonder whether this could be an excuse to divert funds into a new venture. Would it not, I pondered, be possible to create a modern-day equivalent of this exotic Roadster, then use the result as a prototype for further production? As the part owner of a small but prosperous manufacturing company on the northern edge of London, the idea seemed perfectly reasonable – and exciting too.

As I explained the virtues of such a scheme to a number of friends, I received the suggestion from one that the idea must have been "conceived in childhood" and, from another, firm advice that included the word "harebrained". In fact, the more I enthused, the more negative was their attitude and the temptation to abandon any further thoughts was strong indeed. Yet, when another friend suggested that the intended commercial project was merely cover for the fulfilment of a childhood dream, I was more than a little incensed. With a potentially profitable venture in the offing, what did it matter that the auctioneer's postcard was the spark and some part forgotten past obsession the catalyst?

True, from a very early age, my passion for four-wheel vehicles had been stronger than most. In the nineteen-forties, many a happy hour was had with a hand-me-down pedal-car. This was only mildly tempered by the less-than-happy times when left outside some shop or house in the family's elderly airless four-door sedan and told: "Don't move... don't fiddle with anything," and, "We won't be long."

Perhaps our being uprooted from the peaceful English countryside and deposited on a remote farm between Durban and

Pietermaritzburg in South Africa had been a further stimulant. Finding ourselves all of a sudden more preoccupied with snakes and scorpions than with earthworms and robins was a little disturbing to say the least. Moreover, battling up and down rock-strewn hills in an old family Ford and through mud-laden tracks – to say nothing of the traumas of negotiating the ford at the bottom of a gorge – would hardly be considered as keeping pace with the then headlong thrust of world technology.

All too often, the four-wheeled namesake would become hopelessly trapped in the loosely gravelled riverbed. At which, regardless of our attire, out we would clamber and wade splashing towards the bank. After several unsuccessful attempts to extract the car from its watery den, my elder brother would be dispatched the several miles on foot to summon help. He would return an hour or two later with the farm mechanic, the pickup, a suitable number of ropes and chains and, just to be on the safe side, four very large oxen.

At times, we would be on our way within minutes. At others, the farm mechanic and my father would engage in some well-planned antics, ever hopeful of the ensnared vehicle's imminent salvation. The result was usually the same: we were taken home in the back of the pickup and the car followed later, dragged, unceremoniously, by the four oxen.

Could any of this really have a bearing on the design and building of a special car several decades later? My sceptical friends seemed to think so; and possibly my first art teacher would have thought so too:

"Young man," he would say, looking over my shoulder, "can't you draw anything other than cars?" Maybe not, but possibly this early preoccupation might very well have been that spark after all.

Even so, expounding the virtues of a box-cart project, if even jokingly, amongst the more serious aspects of manufacturing a modern-day vehicle was more of an irritant to my late-eighties friends than I realised. All the same, that a gang of us when barely in our teens should have flattened a sheet of corrugated iron with a club hammer to make the body panels for a box-cart, would, I suppose, rate as an early commitment to the cause. In order then to obtain a stylish pattern, that we should dismantle a magnificent wind-up tin-plate toy car and flatten that too, did at least show a sense of destiny: what sacrilege, though, looking back now.

For some reason, the tracings of that poor flattened toy car still exist to this day. Whether kept as proof of an early four-wheeled venture or merely as a reminder of our self-acclaimed great feat of engineering, I have no idea. The result of our endeavours was short lived enough. While testing some modification to the steering, our exotic box-cart ended up semi-disintegrated in a storm water ditch: hard-earned brand new wheels and all.

Of more likely relevance to the present-day scheme, if the remoteness of Africa really had a bearing, was an altogether different vehicle. This truly exotic machine, with its large shining headlamps, narrow split windscreen and rakish flowing wings, was any schoolchild's dream. When first sighted, trunk-lid open and trailer in tow carting chicken manure for a neighbouring farmer, it had been mistaken for one of those car-cum-pickups of the time. Later, this ageing American 'Sixty Special' was entrusted to us as an educational aid for our school. Thus, an aptly named 'Chicken Manure Special' became the 'Motor Club Special', and I, as *finder,* became *keeper* during the holidays.

What we learned with club or car, none of us was ever sure. Certainly, during one long hot African summer, we learned that twelve miles to the gallon could, for no apparent reason, become two and, just as mysteriously, fuel gauges could cease to work altogether. No one, other than the young would-be mechanics, was surprised when several of us found ourselves stranded in the middle of a sugar plantation with a blocked fuel line and a full tank of petrol.

Resorting to the only reasoned way of returning home, one of us sat astride the engine compartment pouring siphoned fuel directly into the air-intake, while another, well ensconced within the safety of the cab, pressed the starter. With a crack and a bang, the engine came to life, the crack aimed back at the pourer and the bang reverberating deep down within the exhaust system. Eventually, a large and elderly engine was coaxed into permanent life, and off we set.

As we sped between the flowing shafts of sugar cane and later through the overhanging branches of the wattle planta-tions, we discovered that, as long as the driver kept the engine fair roaring – either by slipping the clutch or by keeping to lower gears – the engine neither had the time nor the ability to backfire in the pourer's direction. Back home, everything still worked – clutch, gears, engine and brakes – and so, miraculously, did we.

I suppose, if nothing else, such inane behaviour helped develop a sense of ingenuity and improvisation. It also established that luck was likely to play as much a part for a team of late-eighties would-be motor manufacturers in England as it had for some marauding teenagers in early-sixties Africa. That said, the flattening of a sheet of corrugated iron with a club hammer and pouring fuel down an open intake when on the move would, in anyone's estimation, qualify as harebrained – if not downright stupid.

Yes, I could see the thinking behind my friend's disparaging remarks. We were now in high-tech England in the nineteen-eighties, not in the wilds of Africa in the nineteen-fifties and sixties. So, if I was to convince a team of engineers and specialised manufacturers of the sense of launching into a modern-day motor project, such stories were best left untold and flippant attitudes curtailed.

In other words, I had better stick firmly to the realities of conven-tional engineering and good modern-day business sense. An early and valuable lesson had been learned and, duly chastened, I went in search of those who might join such a scheme.

2. Questionable Logic

Jack was an accomplished precision engineer in his mid-thirties who had set himself up in the small industrial town of Haverhill making parts for a wide range of companies, ours included. Of average build and height, Jack was as precise by nature as he was by trade. His pride and joy – bought just before the recent price upsurge – was a DB6 Aston Martin. A committed enthusiast, he would be invaluable on any team.

"Jack, what do you think of this?" I asked, holding out the postcard.

"That's what I call a true classic... it's a Mercedes 540K Special Roadster isn't it?"

"Yes," I replied, "and it's also a rust-heap and the auctioneers think it will sell for more than a million dollars!" At which, in order to get an instant reaction, I added: "What would you think about making something similar... but more usable?"

He went silent for a while. Then, as a concerned frown settled across his forehead: "How would you aim to do that?"

"So you don't think it's impossible?" I part stated, part asked – never forgetting the all too negative reactions of my friends.

Again, a pause: "Well, in mechanical terms nothing is impossible... but it can get very expensive."

Jack was right and, while he might not have confirmed or denied the idea's sanity, he was, as always, suitably cautious. Still, if someone was going to pay the equivalent of several new Rolls-Royces for a run-down antique Mercedes Roadster, was it not reasonable to assume that someone else would be prepared to pay as much as half a Rolls-Royce for a modern exotic, properly drivable similar-styled car? There were already a number of low production specials that partly fitted the description, one or two costing even more.

As we started down our questionable course, why, we pondered, build something from scratch? Some very clever engineers with vast expert backup and huge budgets had already designed the best cars. Surely, with a bit of ingenuity, a team of us enthusiasts and practical engineers could convert and adapt an existing car?

Jack, while retaining his semi-frown, launched into some of the typical problems of older body styles on modern running gear, in particular that of wheel size in relation to body size. If the wheels are too small in comparison to the body, the result always somehow looks unbalanced.

With this one important fact in mind, we both wandered outside to measure up some everyday cars to see how they might fare. We checked their wheelbase in relation to their wheel diameter and compared this against the same ratio of wheelbase to wheel-size of the 540K. Surprisingly, in several instances, the ratio was very similar, albeit the Mercedes being about twenty percent larger overall. Therefore, in theory at least, a scaled down version of something similar to the 540K might in fact be feasible.

Over the next couple of weeks, with "eight hundred thousand pounds, sir," ringing sweetly in our ears, Jack and I continued our evaluations, meeting at his factory when company work was involved or after hours when not.

Our overall theory was to take a normal saloon, and, having discarded the outer skin, somehow squeeze the denuded four-door body backward into a narrower two-door; then, having moved the engine and radiator back, clothe the whole lot in new old-fashioned panelling. While doing this, it should be possible to lighten the car and lower its centre of gravity – especially if the clothes were in aluminium.

The idea came together in fits and starts and, at the time, seemed perfectly sensible. We even discussed how to set up a production run after the prototype. With hindsight, that had to have been a case of extreme ignorance verging on utter bliss. To be discussing making more of some exotic machine when we had barely produced the basis of a theory, to say nothing of the fact that neither of us had been in the motor industry, had to be foolhardy to say the least.

Undeterred, we continued to record the dimensions of several relevant everyday cars while, evening after evening, I put pencil to paper on rough plans – the childhood drawing of cars returning with ease. With the picture on the postcard as a starting point, our evocative thirties-style Roadster began to take shape. As we three-dimensionally juggled the modern components as best possible to fit the flowing lines, the true extent of the project's feasibility began to emerge. This was the Roadster-to-be at its conception: no full-blown drawing office, no elaborate plans, just a couple of over-optimistic enthusiasts working with seat-of-the-pants calculations.

A week later, a Saturday morning, while out mowing the lawn, an elderly Jaguar sweeps into our drive. Out gets a tall, smartly dressed, slightly balding man in his early fifties. He strides towards me, hand thrust in my direction, a broad smile on his face.

"I'm Bruce, I've come about the Roadster project... Jack told me all about it."

He pauses, shakes my hand with a good firm grip, and continues: "From what I hear, this Roadster idea sounds a great challenge. I've always been interested in designing cars and I would very much like to help." Hesitatingly, he adds: "Purely voluntary mind you."

I soon discovered that Bruce at one time had been involved with a range of children's quarter-scale cars. Perhaps he too had been overly inspired from a very early age. Maybe, but I had still not forgotten the reactions of my friends and was not about to admit to disintegrated box-carts or the like. Anyway, on his "purely voluntary" terms, how could we possibly refuse?

"Yes, of course," I said. "We could do with any amount of help... heaven knows, we'll need it."

We quickly discussed what Jack and I had been up to, he complimenting a number of our ideas while criticising others, before he threw in some of his own. He left after an hour, agreeing to drop in to help with the plans a couple of evenings a week.

On each subsequent visit, he brought along a selection of pictures for ideas, then stood over me as I worked. He suggested this change here and that alteration there, often indicating a line was too short or some curve too tight. Most important, he always gave a frank opinion, good or bad. His input proved invaluable.

The next stage would be to find somebody capable of cutting-up and re-welding the body structure as we intended. If done properly, the result would be stronger than the original; but, if done badly, it could prove lethal. Therefore we required someone with a proven track record and, as with any such speculative venture, someone who would do the work at a sensible price.

Jack suggested I visit Des, a local panel beater, while warning me – as he modestly put it – that he could be "a little awkward". Des had moved out of London some years earlier and set up a body repair shop barely a block away from Jack. On arrival, I found myself face to face with a slightly built, wiry individual with all-white hair that belied his younger years. Dressed in a pair of old overalls open to the waist, revealing rough jeans and T-shirt underneath, he exuded an air of laid-back confidence accompanied by a look of benign suspicion.

Concerned not to start off on the wrong foot, half amusingly, I plunged straight in with: "If I brought along something like this," I said, pointing to my middle-aged largish family car, "could you cut it up and weld it back together in a slightly different way?"

"What... what would you want to do that for?" he asked, screwing up his eyes, his gaze darting from side to side as though some candid camera was hiding nearby. Then: "What's wrong with the way it is?"

On reflection, without further explanation, the request must have sounded a bit odd.

"We're thinking of building something like this, out of something like that," I said, smiling as benevolently as possible, while producing the postcard and pointing back at the car. "We've done some initial checks and it seems possible."

He looked at me as though I was completely mad. Then, seeing that I was unmoved and waiting for an answer, his benign suspicion changed to a half-smile and knowing look, no doubt recalling excite-ments of earlier times. Des, I later discovered, was the 'Cockney

Sparrow', a one-time customiser and racer of Austin Minis.

"You're serious, aren't you," he says, studying the postcard and the car. "Well, it'll cost you.... and first you'll have to strip the whole thing out, right down to the bare metalwork."

"You mean you can do it? Cut this off here" – pointing to the wind-screen – "and narrow the front, then put the whole lot back roughly where the front seats are instead?"

"I can do anything if you pay," he retorts. Then adds with a grin: "If it's legal, of course!"

We chatted away, swapping odd stories, especially as an earlier job of mine had involved Minis too. Slowly he warmed; and our eventual parting was with the sure belief that I would return: enthusiasm, it would appear, was as contagious as it was all consuming. For all that, I will forever wonder who encouraged whom.

Were we, though, the remotest bit sensible continuing down such an uncharted path with such uncharted characters? At least Jack's sober, solid and unexcitable attitude, although always suitably positive, was a steadier, and for that I felt easier.

So, the precision engineer, the sometimes car-maker, a potentially irritable panel beater and I, the instigator and drawer of plans, now found ourselves confronted with a multitude of ideas of how to combine drivability, comfortability and usability with a classic thirties look. Jack, Bruce and I ran through many an option, checking the plusses and minuses of each, while often drawing on our respective motoring experiences.

Jack, quite naturally, was keen on all aspects of his beloved DB6 Aston Martin, and Bruce, who at one time had owned an old Bentley, constantly extolled the many virtues of these and its companion car, the Rolls-Royce.

By chance, when in Africa, I too had been involved with the inner workings of an old Rolls-Royce. This much used, mid-thirties classic – known simply by its chassis number of 158 PY – had been bought as a PR tool for the company for which I worked. As the sole but eager volunteer, the task of keeping the elderly giant on the road had fallen to me; and when needs be, a young and newly-betrothed better half, who cared little for the *foreign* car that I then drove, was volunteered too. Indeed, when it came to replacing the carpets and the headlining, she set to with such dedication that the result was later commended by the professionals as being "as professional as the professionals", which was more than anyone had ever said about my endeavours on the mechanical side.

In fact, such was my concern when 158 PY's clutch developed a severe shudder that I begged the help of a marine engineer and a precision toolmaker. Somehow, the unlikely combination did work and, while carrying out the necessary repairs, we discovered, much to our understandable surprise, the clutch plate to be a modified 'best Sheffield' circular-saw blade blank, complete with radial cut-outs to counter heat distortion. So, we all three back then, just as we all three now, came to the conclusion that, provided the reasoning was sound, "anything goes" in engineering, Rolls-Royce, Bentley or whatever.

Bruce immediately went on to extol one other feature on those great cars: the view from behind the steering wheel, that never-ending bonnet hiding a massive engine, guided by an elegant mascot out front, giving a feeling of being a true king of the road.

"Yes, it has to be!" he exclaimed. "We are all children at heart. You know, if..."

"Speak for yourself," interjected Jack with a scowl, stopping Bruce in his tracks. "Let's be serious. We first need to consider..." and he launched into one of his complex mechanical theories.

Despite their long-standing friendship, the all-round innately precise Jack seemed to be permanently at odds with the tall, often flamboyant Bruce. Eventually I came to terms with this unpredictable semi-aggressive banter.

When the two of them had settled their differences, the conversation veered back onto Jack's DB6. Co-incidentally, I too, some years earlier, had succumbed to a similar temptation. However, while Jack's acquisition was recent and costly, mine had been in the early seventies fuel crisis, when these four-litre petrol-eaters were selling for less than Austin Minis.

At the time, the suggestion that this would be a good long-term investment fell on less than receptive ears. A young mother considered there to be more important things on which to spend meagre family funds. Still, with persistence, a very third-hand DB5 Aston Martin was soon to grace the drive of our garageless home.

At sight and sound of new machine, 'the less receptive ears' declined to sit behind the wheel. "It's far too powerful," she repeated time and again, continuing to question the wisdom of such a purchase.

Then, as winter turned to spring and engines warmed and oils thinned, the smoke discharged from the exhaust and the rattle emitted from low down under the bonnet could not be written off to "it'll settle down with time". Eventually, with a borrowed service manual, the assistance of the engineering teacher at a nearby school and the use of the greenhouse – normally the sole preserve of the one who was now not best pleased – a hoped-for cure was under way.

While teacher and pupil attempted to understand the intricacies of double overhead camshafts, Phosphor-Bronze bearings and triple SU carburettors, to say nothing of removable cylinder liners, it was a case of the visually impaired leading the semi-blind. Still, after much head-scratching and knuckle-bareing, a sweet-sounding burble exuded once more from the exhaust: smoke-free and rattle-free to boot.

Now we could put the rejuvenated tear-away through its proper paces. Well, not so: when asked to show its immense power and super versatility, our overhauled engine spluttered and coughed, misfired and backfired. After adjusting some of the simpler settings to no avail, we were left with only one conclusion: the triple carburettors. Yet, for all our fiddling, no sooner had we cured one problem than we seemed to create another; and, in time, I was left to *fiddle* on my own.

As spring gave way to summer, the fiddling continued and the great car's performance gradually improved. Then, returning from work one evening in a company car, I spied heading towards me in the distance a similar Aston to ours. "That's nice," I thought, "to see a DB 4, 5 or 6 out being enjoyed" – all three being similar head-on and from afar. The car disappeared into a dip, only to reappear on the brow just ahead. As it came over the rise, the body rose into the air and the wheels fell away from underneath.

"Good grief", I muttered to myself, as it flew past with a thunderous roar, "they're gunning it".

By chance, I caught a glimpse of the passenger, ashen-faced and white-knuckled, gripping the panic handle on the dashboard. There, nose halfway to the windscreen, was my young brother-in-law. What I had just seen was *our* car; and there could only be *one* driver.

The words that passed between husband and wife a short while later were a trifle more than a little interesting, and negotiations to borrow greenhouses have proved easier ever since.

"No, it's far too powerful," – some chance.

Finally, that long awaited trial was savoured and enjoyed – and I wholly understood Jack's feelings. Apart from its breathtaking straight-line performance, the elegant brute could be thrown around corners at an incredible speed: maybe not as easily or as fast as modern, lighter cars, but fast enough. Added to that, the latest in disc brakes certainly knew how to bring it to a halt, which was more than could be said for antique Rolls-Royces or some of those American cars in Africa.

As Jack, Bruce and I ended our discussion, we knew the Roadster's benchmarks had been set. The likes of the Rolls and the Bentley, with the obvious excellence of engineering, along with the majesty of an elegant bonnet aimed by an emblem way out front, would represent the epitome of luxury; the Aston Martins, with their power, good handling and sheer thrill, would symbolise the fun element; and, just for good measure, all the push-buttons associated with the best of the Americans should be there too.

Therefore, like some giant cooking recipe, we were somehow going to mix the best attributes of all such ultimate cars and there, miraculously, we would have our Roadster. Whether or not this was arrived at through ignorance, arrogance or a combination of both, or merely because those 'anything goes' late nineteen-eighties had turned us light-headed, we will never be sure.

Be that as it may, our Roadster, of necessity, would have to be its *own* car with its *own* characteristics and of a make still to be decided; and, with these apparently trivial facts yet to be established, we continued into the lion's den.

3. An Idea Evolves

Frank was a jolly, generous-hearted farmer in his mid-fifties whose family had worked their Suffolk farm for several generations. Mainly arable, being typical of the area, Frank was also heavily into fresh turkeys, with shed upon shed of the essential Christmas fare being produced in the run up to the festive season. Introduced by Bruce, Frank was another Aston Martin enthusiast, having for many years owned one of the first of the famous DB4, 5 and 6 trio.

Another Aston: an omen maybe, I thought? More to the point, I suspect, was that a group of middling-aged men had become dedicated to a particular middling-aged mechanical art form. Frank, connoisseur to the last, proved an excellent additional critic. Unlike Bruce, who always gave an instant opinion, Frank would stand well back, study the plans through a semi-permanent frown, and only comment when quite sure he had fully thought things through. Also, very conveniently, Frank had a large redundant barn where the project could start – if start it ever did.

"Whether you decide on a convertible or a fixed top, you're going to have trouble with the handling," said our newfound team member one evening, when he, Bruce, Jack and I had gathered in his comfortable farmhouse. He went on: "It's a known fact that thirties-style cars don't handle well. Their open front wings allow them to twist and flex. You'll lose all consistency, especially with modern suspension."

Bruce looked blankly at farmer Frank and said nothing, no doubt suspecting he was being a little overly academic. Having already discovered from other sources that Frank was not being quite so pedantic, I threw in an idea of my own: "What if we were to combine the stiffness of the monocoque construction around the cab, with some sort of space-frame arrangement out front? Would that not produce the necessary rigidity?"

"That's clever," Bruce said, without a second thought.

"Maybe," interjected Jack, not wanting to commit to something plucked from thin air, his solid engineering coming to the fore. "Theories are one thing, but practicalities can be quite another. Anyway, it will all depend on the actual car used. Until that's decided, we'll never be sure what is and what isn't possible."

He was of course right: we had to decide. Ideally, we wanted something reliable with good handling and, preferably, a machine that was easy to service and maintain. In addition, if we wished to benefit from a prestige name, we also required a marque with a long and suitably exotic history.

I had long since favoured a world-famous make that originated from well beyond our shores. How, though, would I convince a group of patriotic Englishmen to use something *foreign*? I certainly had my reasons, but any persuasive arguments were not of a textbook nature and originated in other places at other times. So, whenever the opportunity arose, I discreetly related incidents and facts that I hoped might sway them to my way of thinking.

In particular was the time in the mid-seventies when I went on an assignment to Dubai in the United Arab Emirates, with the family intent on joining me several months later. Considering the expense, our telephone conversations back then, although regular, were generally short. One, in particularly, I remember well.

"You'll like the car I've bought you," I said. "It's bright green with a broad white stripe down each side. It's got a large powerful V8 engine and has manual gears."

What I omitted to say was that the manual gears were not five-speed floor-shift like her 'flying' Aston, but basic three-speed with the lever on the steering column. In addition, the so-called *little* Oldsmobile was very second hand and known around Dubai as the 'Green Mamba' – named after that infamous African snake of which none of us had been particularly fond when there.

When eventually all together again, ensconced in our desert home with flat roof, noisy air-conditioning and over-large, anti-glare windows, I imparted some hints as to the intricacies of driving a *foreign* car in this newly expanding *foreign* land. The column-shift gears were soon mastered. Conquering some of the local terrain, however, took a little longer.

"All the tyres have gone flat!" I was angrily informed on the telephone, as I sat one morning minding my own business at the office.

Disbelief gave way to suspicion; but still the 'knight in shining armour' headed to the rescue. When I arrived, there, alongside the concrete drive up to its axles in our sandpit of a garden, was the

Mamba. I dug away at one of the wheels – suitably assisted by two small children – to expose a perfectly well blown up tyre. As we dug away at the other three, which were to prove no different, I pondered whether perhaps the firmly embedded wheels were not just retribution for the airborne ones a couple of years earlier.

A friendly Arab, working with a front-end loader nearby, was soon coaxed to the rescue. His metal-toothed monster, as though picking up some twig, manoeuvred the Mamba by its bumpers back onto the concrete drive: from where it should never have been removed other than to drive out of the gate. As I watched, fascinated, I began to feel there was something rather appealing about these cars. The sheer brutishness of being manhandled by a bit of earth-moving equipment, with no apparent ill effects, was an unexpected revelation.

As I relayed such tales a decade or more later to Jack, Bruce and Frank – and occasionally to Des – I made sure not to omit stories of that other desert Oldsmobile, the company's 'Delta 88'. With its even larger V8 engine and capable of seating four astride each of its bench seats fore and aft, the 88 was the epitome of nineteen-seventies comfort. Such luxuries in those early pioneering days were always well received, as to get from one place to another was often complicated and hazardous to say the least. Roads could appear with no warning as easily as they could disappear without trace.

"New tarred road open to Al Ain," leapt off the pages of the local press one day. This one-hundred-mile direct route to the inland town had only ever been passable with four-wheel drive and the alternative tarred route was more than twice the distance. As a colleague and I needed to get to Al Ain for a meeting, we could at least use the 88, with its air-conditioning and many other comforts as kindly supplied by Detroit, to say nothing of saving hours of wasted travel time.

The road heading inland out of Dubai stretches into the middle-distance up towards the hills, the landscape steadily changing from flatter, harder rock-filled terrain to undulating dunes. Some sand had blown onto the tar but, with the power of the massive engine and a sturdy two-and-half tons, we roared along with ease. We chatted together, idling away the time, while keeping an eye out for camels and those other ever-present desert hazards, goats.

Suddenly there was nothing; the road just disappeared. We were doing about eighty miles an hour and it simply vanished. There were just sand dunes and tracks.

As we hit the first dune – all of two feet high – the front-end lifted, sand scattering like smoke. We listened for the sound of wrenched-back wheels or grating fan on radiator. I could visualise being stuck here, waiting in the raging heat, ever hopeful, hour upon hour, of imminent rescue. I could also imagine certain people being highly unamused at having to piece back together one semi-dismantled company car.

We came crashing down. I jerked the wheel. Luck was with us: the steering still worked and the power was still there too. Then we hit the next dune, only slightly slower but with almost equal force. Again, the front reared, only to crash down and take yet another mouthful of sand. I could barely believe what this smooth-riding luxury machine was withstanding. No normal car could put up with such punishment. Surely, the whole thing would break up at the next bump or jolt?

We dared not stop. We would have sunk to the axles, just as the Mamba had only weeks earlier, and there were no friendly Arabs with front-end loaders out here. Neither of us spoke, other than for one of us to curse whoever had claimed the road to be complete. We ploughed on, mile after mile, sure that our luck could not hold.

It did; and, as mysteriously as it had disappeared, the fresh black surface reappeared and, with a leap and a bump, we were back on a smooth solid surface once more.

We arrived in Al Ain to head for the nearest hotel to calm our shaken bodies and soothe our shattered nerves. The answer as to why someone had claimed the road to be complete when it was so obviously not was quick enough in coming, and accompanied by a hearty laugh: neither of the adjoining Sheikhs would admit to owning the bordering stretch of useless land. In other words, it was typical of a border dispute at the time, but in reverse.

We took the long way back to Dubai.

On our return, a thorough check of the 88 found little of concern. Certainly, the underside had been well sandblasted and the front bumper showed every sign of having taken the full force of those dunes but, apart from that, nothing seemed the worse for wear and not a drop of anything had been lost.

I had to marvel at the indestructibility of those desert Oldsmobiles; as did someone else, someone who now decided she quite liked these *foreign* machines after all. So, on returning to England, a much-loved Aston Martin, its reliability somewhat the worse for age, was replaced by a middle-aged, wide-eyed semi-sporting Chevrolet – a lowly but dependable cousin to the two Oldsmobiles.

To our amusement, on its very first outing to our children's school, a fellow parent remarked: "Your car looks like a shark, just like Jaws." And the name Jaws stuck.

On reflection, by gracing the doorsteps of rural England, especially back then, with something considered to have come from another planet was bound to stir emotions. Moreover, when a more conservative second-hand Seville – as manufactured by Cadillac, that senior brother to all Oldsmobiles and Chevrolets – replaced the wide-eyed car, the name Jaws continued.

This 1976-'79 machine was unlike any other medium-to-large car I had driven. There was no excessive roll or wallow and for a so-called, by American standards, 'compact', it was heavy – the ride told you that. Yet, despite this, the steering was light – but still with adequate feel – and it appeared neither to oversteer nor understeer, giving surprisingly good handling.

The true extent of this, we only discovered by chance while staying with friends for the christening of one of their children. Mid-morning, the conversation was abruptly broken by: "We're going to be late." We, the members of the congregation coming from the west of Scotland – which included the child – were going to be late for the christening some forty miles to the east.

When, with another couple, we found ourselves in the Seville in the middle of a three-car convoy, I enquired where we were going. Nobody knew, nor did they think anyone in the car behind knew. The only people evidently who did were the parents of the child, and they were in a modern turbo-something rapidly disappearing around a corner up ahead.

"Follow that child!" we roared in unison, like Keystone Kops of old. No amount of flashing lights would slow the turbo-something, and the drive from west to east was the most hair-raising ever encountered. Corners came and went, hills seemed to change from up to down when least expected and sheep, ready to leap out without warning, were a hazard I could have done without. For what seemed an eternity, the passengers, in stunned silence, swayed from side to side and back and forth, stabilised only by the armrests to their sides and the panic-handles above. I clung to the steering wheel as best I could, violently swinging one way and the other, while all the time concentrating on the turbo-something steaming along ahead.

Somehow, and in one piece, we 'got to the church on time'. Then, after the service, while venting our none-too-happy feelings on the father of the child, the owner of the third car, itself something compact and powerful, bore witness to the Seville's performance. "Never," he said, "have I seen a car remotely the size of yours take corners like that. I only just managed to keep up because I too had no idea where we were going!"

The father of the child, while claiming that he thought someone knew the way, had assumed that our flashing lights were for him to go faster. Such reasoning, we agreed without exception, was unfath-omable; but at least we had survived.

As the years passed, we came to know and understand this compact, complex car for what it was. Features were fitted that are still not on cars to this day. For all that, seldom did anything go wrong; and I often thought: "How could anyone make anything better, maybe less complex and more economical, but not really better?" On the other hand, the continued enjoyment, year after year, of our ageing metal steed might mean that we were becoming a little fossilised in our middle years. Whether this was true or not, these indestructible giants, and in particular the Seville with its multitude of miles travelled, had more than withstood the tests of time.

That, together with the marque's long history dating back to 1902, its legendary nineteen-thirties' V16s, tail-finned glamour-wagons of the fifties and sixties and grand presidential transport of the seventies and eighties, was surely testimony enough for my preference. Added to that, the late-seventies Seville's compact wheelbase and it being rear wheel drive conformed exactly to our requirements. Of equal importance, all the Seville's special features are separate and repairable. Often, a small individual piece could be replaced to rectify some function and, apart from the electronic fuel injection and one or two other non-essential features, there was a complete absence of computerisation. In other words, everything was repairable by the average 'repairers of cars' – us included.

I had one last ruse that should further help convince the others. I had discovered that a number of items on the Seville were used on some very up-market domestic cars. The V12 Jaguar, for one, was fitted with the same three-speed automatic transmission; and one or two other UK makes used a variety of components also sourced from General Motors USA.

Finally, as the one whose company would be funding the project, I would have thought that I was entitled to the greatest say. Under normal circumstances, yes; but I was fast learning that these were not normal circumstances and that they were unlikely to become any more so as the project proceeded. All the same, with a few more questions and answers, I believed I could convince the rest of the team of my reasoning.

Bruce was won over quickly enough, no doubt at the thought of doing something out of the ordinary. Jack, solid and reserved as always, was less sure and Frank, with his strong roots to the land, remained sceptical. Des, on the other hand, seemed more concerned about cutting up and welding together something he had never before laid hands on. Still, as he was the one who had said, "I can do anything if it's legal", and as it was Jaws that I had first shown him anyway, I had reason to presume, when the time came, that he could, and would, do as he claimed.

His first reaction, while waving an arm in the general direction of some imported cars littering his yard, was: "Where will you get spares?" To which he followed up with: "These foreign makes take for ever to get things for. Believe me, bits'll get lost, bits'll get broken. You'll see."

Knowing that I already had the support of the excitable but dependable Tom, who had looked after Jaws at the local Rover agency for so long that he barely needed the manuals any more, I explained that all the general wearing parts were available in the UK. As for the more unusual items, we had for some time been importing these from a GM agency in Cleveland, Ohio. Their parts manager, Bob, had always found what was needed and there was no reason to assume any difference now.

Jack raised another point: "How is the Seville perceived by others? People are bound to ask... especially when considering buying a 'modified special'."

Bob in America had already partly answered this. He had somehow managed to dig up a report at the time of the Seville's launch by 'Car and Driver' magazine. Emblazoned on the cover was the headline: "Seville: Cadillac-Rolls with the punches". Inside was a write-up versus the Rolls-Royce Silver Shadow, along with a number of references to the then current Mercedes Benz.

Apart from the admission that the Rolls-Royce was, and most probably always would be, a better car, the Seville on many counts did not come second. A picture of the two standing side by side showed the Seville to be inches lower than the Rolls – roof line bonnet and floor pan – but, for all that, the Seville's outer track was wider than that of the Rolls. This effectively lower roll centre combined with a lower floor pan helped explain how GM had achieved good handling while still providing a comfortable, more upright seating position. This also explained why our favoured machine would never be the best of off-roaders.

One vital question remained: would we be allowed to retain the prestigious name, especially if we were to change the style and structure as drastically as we envisaged? Bruce, who had raised the subject with monotonous regularity, brought it up one evening yet again. Frank, in obvious frustration, made a simple suggestion.

"Why don't you telephone GM and ask them? At least you'll get an idea of their attitude and then decide one way or the other what to do." After which, he drew a measured breath and added: "They can't sue you for telephoning them, now can they?"

The task fell to me. On returning home, I obtained the GM number in Detroit from directory enquiries, and dialled. I had little success at first, other than: "Sir, all product liability will cease as soon as you modify anything," or, "Sir, I am unable to give you a categorical answer to such a question." Eventually, perseverance paid off and I was put through to someone who seemed well versed with the 'likes of us' wishing to cut up that made by the 'likes of them'.

The polite GM executive explained in great detail GM's policy towards the customising of cars, finishing off with: "Yes, we are very relaxed about the ongoing use of our name. But may I remind you that we disclaim all liability as soon as anything is modified."

I again questioned how GM could possibly permit the use of their name after such major changes as we intended. Again, he repeated the simple statement: "Once a Seville, always a Seville".

"Yes," I persisted "I accept that, but what we are intending won't end up looking remotely like anything GM has ever made. Are you quite sure it will be OK?"

"Sir," he started, sounding more than mildly frustrated, "let me put it like this. We, at General Motors, could not come to England... buy a Rolls-Royce... bring it back to America... cut it up... put it back together a different way... then call it a Buick." There was a suitable pause, after which he concluded with, "now could we sir?"

Put like that, the point was taken and, after due thanks, he was let off having to put up with any more of my nonsense. Dealing with a nutty bunch of individuals from the old world who had taken it upon themselves to cut up one of your more celebrated models, albeit an older one, was bad enough, but to be argued with over your verdict was, I suppose, somewhat uncalled-for.

Therefore, a late seventies Seville it would be, and apparently legal to boot. Furthermore, providing we looked after old Jaws, we would end up with a 'before' and an 'after' – if, of course, we ever completed what we thought we were about to start.

4. Committed

Our starting point for an outer body that would accommodate the Seville's running gear and modern-day features was the classic lines of the 540K as depicted on the inspirational postcard. We then set about adding ideas from various books, while using every trick possible to hide the 'potential protrusions' of some awkward modern components and making sure to keep an authentic overall thirties flow. We toiled on, evenings and weekends, while intermittently checking measurements on Jaws. Gradually a set of tenth-scale drawings evolved.

"What about the grille?" Bruce asked during one of our meetings, eyeing the blank hole in the centre of the front elevation; no doubt recollecting problems with his own car projects when trying to make a decision on a particular feature.

Often a special identification on older cars, the grille could hardly be a look-alike from the thirties that would insult the collectors of vintage cars. Nor would it be very wise to upset GM by using something that could be construed as out of keeping or possibly reminiscent of another marque.

"What about," Bruce suggested after some thought, "the Seville's own style of grille, but narrower and taller?"

Considering the instant nature of the solution, not surprisingly, I gave Bruce one of Jack's sideways looks and, for a moment at least, remained silent. Then, just as quickly, added: "Well, let's give it a try."

Jack and Frank were instant in their agreement. Des liked the idea too but Des, as we were slowly discovering, would say he liked anything if he thought a challenge was involved. As for GM, we were mindful of the earlier telephone call and decided discretion to be our best course.

Who, we now wondered, could make the aluminium outer body and at what price? To help shortcut this, I contacted the secretary of the Rolls-Royce Enthusiasts Club, who I had known back in the days of 158PY.

"You're thinking of doing *what*?" he said with incredulity. "You've spent time with a genuine thoroughbred vintage car, and you're thinking of making a replica out of a Seville. Have you taken leave of your senses?"

"It's not a *replica*," I retorted, with some irritation. "It is its *own* design and will be its *own* car." I paused for a reply. There being none, I went on: "We're merely borrowing a few of the better ideas from a previous era and combining them to best advantage. Anyway, we're trying to make something more usable. All your older classics have become far too valuable to be driven about just for fun's sake."

After a debate on the old and the not-so-old, and the pure and the not-so-pure, he mellowed, not least when I pointed out that some of his cars had bits of GM in them anyway; to which he naturally put up an honourable defence. In the end, he promised to send a copy of the club's latest advertising supplement and, much to my surprise, even wished us luck.

A week or so later, during one of our afternoon discussions, Jack, no doubt in order to keep us on our toes, posed the question: "Are you sure it shouldn't be a convertible? People will want to be seen out and about, and feel the wind in their faces?"

While I tried gently to steer him away from the temptations and complications of a convertible, Bruce reacted rather more forcefully.

"How many convertible Ferraris have you seen?" he retorted, scowling at Jack. "And, anyway, those that you have seen have mostly had their roofs chopped off afterwards." To which, he followed up, both barrels firing: "Ferraris don't make convertibles because convertibles don't drive properly... and we want this car to drive properly."

With that, there was no more discussion on convertibles and we soon settled down to the more humdrum matters at hand.

Then, as Jack, Bruce and I were poring over the plans at yet another session, Jack, with apparent seriousness, came up with: "What about the children?"

"What do you mean?" I enquired, taken aback.

"Well, people will want to take their children on family outings, won't they? Where are the children going to sit... what about a 'dickey' or 'rumble' seat?"

"Ferraris don't have dickey seats," retorted Bruce, with a certain incredulity. "*They* don't cater for children, so why should we?"

The two of them were at it again: Bruce and his racing Ferraris and Jack and his family jaunts. What with Bruce having never had anything to do with Ferraris, and Jack's distinctly un-family-like pride and joy, I wondered from where their motives sprang. Nothing I said change this continual differing vision of the end product. The two them had known each other far longer than I had known either, so I decided to stay well out of the affray and kept my gaze firmly fixed on the plans, waiting for the impasse to end.

Such an idea was quite out of the question: there was simply not enough room to sit in the cab in the two massive armchair seats and end up with anything more than a barely adequate trunk behind. So, whether we liked it or not, the total carrying capacity of our mighty machine would be no more than two people and a suitcase; and, for all Jack's concern, that was that.

All we appeared to lack now was a qualified professional motor engineer to guide us through some of the more intricate hurdles. However, when Sandy, a qualified structural engineer, threw caution to the wind and joined in, we decided there were enough engineers to be going on with. Sandy, late-thirties with a modern factory that included a plethora of facilities for commercial vehicle fabrication, would have most answers relating to the structural stresses within a modern vehicle. Besides, he always found time to talk things through and he always bubbled over with confidence and enthusiasm.

To further reduce any lingering concerns about this lack of a motor professional, we discovered a book called 'Designing and Building Special Cars'. The author did not go so far as to explain how to cut up and reposition items quite to the extent that we intended – no doubt he was eminently sane. Nevertheless, the book did explain, in general terms at least, what was feasible, along with numerous do's and don'ts and many detailed formulae.

So, rightly or wrongly, the team decided a qualified motor engineer would be best kept away from what a group of amateurs were up to, or at least until the basic alterations had been completed. By that time, there would at least be something to show for all our theory.

At this point, with the welcome offer from a self-professed 'single-handed Back-up', the one who had originally said "what a good idea", that she would do the 'backing up' – especially where 'sustenance' was concerned – we decided it was time to put a proposal to the company. In retrospect, our list of specifications was outlandish enough for any vehicle conversion, but for the handling and road holding to be "as good if not better", as Bruce was intent on, had to be a little over the

...ight a team of amateur auto-engineers, especially ...tests, were going to achieve this, I have no idea. ...ould appear, was beginning to outweigh common ...nd growing factor.

...excel even further when setting a budget for our ... supercar. To cover the second-hand Seville with all its necessa.., parts, the special thirties-style body and fitments and the estimated fifteen hundred man-hours of modification and construction time, we allocated no more than the price of a modern mid-to-high-range luxury car. In our ever-growing euphoria, we concluded that the design and management would merely be absorbed within the normal running of the company. Such *rational* commercial economics could only have been founded on the boom-time philosophy that prevailed at the time.

There were two requests from other shareholders: firstly, that the company's patented 'frictionless' hinges be included in the final design and, second, that there should be an early cut-off point at which we would either abandon the project or, come hell what may, be sure to proceed to completion. We quickly agreed to both: the unusual hinges would somehow be found somewhere suitable, and the cut-off point we decided would coincide with the inaugural visit of a fully-qualified motor engineer.

Thus, a mere six weeks after receiving the auctioneer's postcard, Bruce and I found ourselves heading south to inspect a second-hand 1978 Seville, the same as Jaws.

"The Seville's such a lovely car, drives so beautifully," the super-positive voice had purred down the telephone. "It's been exceptionally well looked after." Then, presumably for good effect: "It was owned by a well-known woman in television, you know."

"Yes, good... and what about the interior?" We had enquired, ignoring the insinuated 'little old lady' syndrome.

"The interior's quite perfect... beautiful black leather... quite exquisite."

That was particularly useful, as an all-black interior would go well with any exterior colour we might decide on.

He went on: "The whole car is mechanically perfect. I believe the engine's had a complete overhaul."

For my part, I sincerely hoped the engine had not had an overhaul.

By the sound of the over-exuberant salesman, the insides of the engine could have benefited about as much as the Motor Club Special had when maintained by us at school.

"And the exterior, what's that like?"

"Oh, that's very good... well, there're a few blemishes, the odd mark."

That probably meant the outside was decidedly rough. Good, we thought, that should help with the price and, while making a date for a visit, finished off with: "But we think you're asking too much."

"We can talk, we can talk," he had concluded.

We arrived to find our potential purchase securely boxed in at the back of an over-cluttered showroom. The battery was flat, one or two of the tyres were rather lower on pressure than needed for comfort and the friendly salesman was surprised to see us.

"Don't worry," he said, "we'll have everything sorted out in a moment... isn't she beautiful?"

No, I thought to myself, she is not beautiful. Not only was the body grazed down both sides with bits of trim peeling off, but the wing mirrors were rather more adjustable than originally intended. Presumably, someone had been trying to squeeze this not-too-small car into a not-too-large British garage. In addition, the same person or possibly someone else had been over-energetic with the polishing and had removed most of the paint from the sharper edges of its angular seventies body.

That we would be discarding the outside panelling was best left unsaid. For one thing, there would probably be one of Des's 'where's the camera' acts and, for another, and more to the point, I doubt this purveyor of automobiles would brook any bargaining.

He was right about the interior, though: the jet-black leather looked almost new and the trim and fittings were the same. When eventually extracted from the showroom and taken for a drive, the car felt like the well run-in, under-stressed machine that it undoubtedly was. Indeed, in the absence of any documented evidence, we doubted the smooth-running power plant had ever been opened.

Accordingly, Seville, registration HLN 827V, became ours to drive away. At this, Bruce, with a caution seldom normally displayed, insisted on trailing me home, fearful our new acquisition might falter on the way.

While heading north and eyeing Bruce in the rear-view mirror, a continual slight swaying caused by worn shock absorbers reminded me of something I had conveniently been putting to the back of my mind. Now, having committed hard cash to our course of action, the 'something', very inconveniently, was beginning to rear its head.

It harked back to the demise of an elderly but much-cherished vehicle that had been bought to ferry us between the university campus at the top of the hill in Pietermaritzburg and our lodgings in the town centre below. Known simply as the University Buick, we employed every possible tactic to keep it on the road. The topping up of old-time shock absorbers with water rather than with unaffordable oil was the one such tactic now tugging at my memory. Surprisingly, the idea had worked remarkably well and the roller-coaster ride experienced when travelling much over thirty miles an hour was permanently cured.

Another problem, a badly worn timing chain proved more challenging, especially on a Saturday when the local breakers yard, our normal source of spares, was closed. In desperation, someone suggested shortening the chain by removing a link and tying the ends together with thick fencing wire. With no better idea, we set to doing just that. Then, after negotiating with the 'keeper of the boiler-house' to use the only available furnace-type heat to temper the wire to give it added strength – and after a number of burnt fingers had been crudely bandaged – the chain was returned to the engine from where it had come. We went on our Saturday night outing and, miraculously, we got back again too.

Such ingenuity, though, was not enough to save our cherished machine. Besides, the girls became increasingly suspicious that the old car's refusal to restart halfway through an evening was deliberate. Finally, when driving uninvited on the local racetrack to *test* some improvement we had made to the engine, the University Buick, in a travesty of mechanical disasters, simply died.

As Bruce and I continued northwards, I became ever more conscious of what we had done next all those years ago: in a way funny, but very stupid really. To have bought a vehicle, however affordable, that no girl was prepared to ride in, day or night, was not the best of ploys. A large and ageing hearse, with the acquired motto of "where the dead lay, the living now play", was hardly conducive to a romantic evening out.

It was what then followed that was now causing me even more serious twinges; little voices inside saying: "beware!" As a bunch of apparently sane university students, we somehow became convinced that the only solution to our predicament was to build our own car, and a stylish sports-car at that. With our then-considered superior intellect, we were sure any obstacle, however great, was conquerable.

"How about a mixture between a Ferrari and a Corvette?" someone suggested.

The fact that Ferraris, Corvettes and other such exotic cars were virtually unheard of in Africa at the time – other than in films and magazines – appeared to be of little consequence. We would obtain an old chassis with an American V8 engine, plenty of which were around at the time, either through age or accidents. We would carry out the alterations with cutting and welding gear, and make a new body using tubular framework covered in sheet metal or fibreglass.

As the willing drawer-of-cars, I started on the plans. The Ferrari-cum-Corvette would, quite naturally, be a convertible: we would want everyone to see who was inside. I have no idea how long the drawings took but certainly most were done during lectures. An interesting lecture or an important one and the plans remained unaltered; a boring lecture – interspersed with an occasional "*boy*, are you concen-trating?" – and the plans progressed apace.

At some stage during the design, we came up with a number of so-called brainwaves. One of these theorised that if the majority of the body curves were non-compound – the one-directional curves like the side of a tin can, as against the multi-directional sort such as those of an egg – then ordinary flat sheet metal could be used. We could easily slot in the few essential compound pieces afterwards.

Another brainwave was to have no doors. Car doors, we concluded, were extremely complex and not an essential part of any true sports-car. However, to have climbed through the minute window openings with the roof on, as drawn, was optimistic to say the least. The theory, apparently, was that the roof would hardly ever be on: not too practical with the almost daily summer thunderstorms on the east coast of Africa where we lived.

When by chance we found an almost brand-new V8 engine at a knock down price, we clubbed together and bought it and, with nowhere to store it, put it on the veranda of our lodgings. Thereafter, each week, late in the evening and without any silencers, we *exercised* our new acquisition – to keep it healthy, so we claimed. Looking back, I now understand why the "young man" of my youth had regressed to "boy" in my late teens.

Later, we came across an engineless speedboat. It was summer, the weather was excellent, the boat was on the cheap and we became temporarily deflected from our true purpose. The engine was put in the boat and, for the time being at least, we made use of the undoubted attractions of a semi-reliable speedboat, while continuing to endure our ill-conceived set of wheels. Still, our sports-car would, we claimed, be resurrected when winter set in.

Winter came and an even less reliable speedboat was, at times, to be seen 'bottom up' having its underside repaired and, at others, with 'bottoms up' as the misguided owners attempted to save their mechanical investment from the ravages of seawater. As with most things diverted from their true goal, temporary became permanent and our intended sports-car slipped into oblivion.

Apart from being a lesson on how not to be waylaid by seemingly more attractive propositions, what a waste of all that drawing, calculating and planning. Maybe: but just as the tracings of the flattened wind-up tin-plate toy car from the days on the farm have survived, so too have the plans of the Ferrari-cum-Corvette.

At first glance, the flowing lines and sporty looks bring to light some interesting facts. Certainly bits of Ferrari are recognisable but, other than the windscreen, not much Corvette. Against this, it would seem that, unless our sports-car's suspension had been totally rigid and unmoving, the first bump would have thrown one, if not all the wheels through their respective mudguards and torn both tyres and body-work to shreds.

On closer examination, more is revealed: no normal person could have got into that car, whether the roof was on or off. They might have if there had been no engine to obstruct their legs, but that was yet another problem: the engine would either have had the sump dragging on the ground or its top-end would have obscured the driver's vision. Certainly there are hot-rods with similar features, but we were intent on making a sleek Ferrari-cum-Corvette.

What idiots: all we seemed to have learned back then, at least in engineering terms, was a surfeit of what *not* to do. No wonder these earlier goings-on were returning to haunt me. Writing off a box-cart in a storm-water drain due to childish experiments with the steering is one thing; but for a time-consuming venture at university to usher up such ineptitude was quite another.

Bruce, Jack and the others would, I was sure, have experienced similar escapades in their youth, but I doubted any could have been quite as inane. Frank too, I think, with his naturally sceptical down-to-earth attitude, suspected everything was not quite as it should be; and Des, if he were told of such stupidities, would no doubt give me one of his quizzical looks, of which I could do well without. On the other hand, keeping this incompetence to myself could prove an invaluable asset: a recurring pinprick to think things through in a thorough logical fashion, to check every last aspect, not once but twice or even three times.

As our two-car convoy continued its journey north, I realised that some sort of pinprick had already been at work. Perhaps the university fiasco was having a subconscious effect after all. Sandy and I, even this early on, had already been checking on some of our more unconventional ideas. The crossbar between the wings in front of the grille to take the headlamps was just one such example.

Originally meant solely as decorative support for the headlamps, the bar would now also tie together the front ends of our forward-pointing space-frames on the front of a shortened 'monocoque' – or 'unibody', to which it is often referred. Sandy, with his structural engineering, and I, with my half-remembered theory of the triangle of forces, had therefore managed to conclude the final stage of the inter-locking double-tripod space-frames – and without any unsightly stress bars protruding between bonnet and wings.

We had even solved that other awkward piece of the structural jigsaw: how to support the rear of the transmission within the confines of a narrowed driveline tunnel, while still retaining the rubber-mounted isolation of the Seville's front half-chassis to which the engine, steering and front suspension were attached.

Our answer in this case was a backward-pointing A-frame, the legs of the A being attached to the rear legs of the half-chassis, with the peak of the A held on an extra rubber mount back down the tunnel. The crosspiece of the A would then support the transmission. The frame would be fixed in such a way that the peak of the A could move vertically – so as not to interfere with the overall cushioning of the six existing rubber mounts – but would be rigid horizontally in order to help prevent any rotation of the half-chassis due to it having been shortened at the front.

"What do you think?" Sandy asked, as we ran through the more than mildly convoluted idea, while adding with his usual gusto: "Isn't it great?"

"Seems sensible," I replied with a certain caution, not being in Sandy's league on such matters.

"It's fantastic, it's great... you must think so?" he exuded, continuing with his normal excess and beaming uncontrollably.

Such complex decisions could so easily have been left till later, potentially causing serious complications if they had. So, perhaps some unseen force was keeping us on our toes after all. Despite this, as Bruce and I continued ferrying the object of our imminent motor project nearer home, my concerns persisted. True, on the plus side, some of our theory could be a stroke of creative genius; but, just as easily, our multi-faceted hypotheses could be a case of unadulterated wishful thinking. In other words, what we were launching ourselves into could end up as another Ferrari-cum-Corvette and, of such a debacle, especially in my middling years, I could willingly forgo.

On arriving home, we were met excitedly by a young son wanting to be taken for a ride; supposedly, to be able to say he had been in the car before it had been "cut up". So, having dutifully accommodated the youthful request, I bade Bruce farewell and headed off to deposit our newly purchased plaything in Frank's barn. On the way, I dropped in on Des.

"There she is," I said, as he appeared, sporting his normal inquisitive look. "We'll have it all stripped out and ready for you in no time at all."

"Yes," he said, then, almost as an aside: "I'm going on holiday." Then, after a pause: "I'm not sure when I'll be back."

Ignoring my look of astonishment and pointing into the middle-distance, he calmly added: "Don't worry, he'll sort it all out. He knows what to do... he's my 'number two'."

I stood transfixed. Surely not, I thought. No, there was little point contemplating the possibility of a stripped-out Seville remaining, forever and a day, scattered over Frank's barn. I smiled benignly, wished Des a happy holiday, and made for the barn.

Frank's redundant grain barn, a few miles out of town on a narrow winding road, was approached down a short tree-lined track that quickly opened onto a wide spread of rolling Suffolk and Essex countryside. About sixty feet long by thirty feet wide, the building was one of those multi-age composites constructed mainly of corrugated iron, that old favourite in so many parts of Africa. To the front was an equally large rough concrete forecourt.

Inside, through a pair of large sliding metal doors, was an expanse of concrete floor surrounded by the darkly painted rippled metal walls capped with an equally dark rippled metal roof, all of which were interspersed with the occasional oak beam, presumably from an earlier age. Ahead of the doors and to one side was an extended alcove housing a couple of old flatbed trailers and, to add to its welcoming embrace, some well-aired, dust-inducing eaves were clearly visible on three sides. Such a relic of an older age could hardly be accused of meeting the norms of late twentieth century manufacturing – suffice, it would have to do.

Jack was already there to cast an eye over both barn and purchase. A certain smile of satisfaction, barely visible, spread across his face at the realisation that we had actually made a start. He then presented me with a book.

"It's the history of Cadillac," he said. "It was on special offer. I thought you might like it. There are pictures of all sorts of models, right from the beginning, and up to and including the Seville. Have it as a sort of 'start-up' present."

"Thank you," I said, catching hold of the publication with its large V on the front denoting the marque's long record of V8, V12 and V16 engines.

That evening, idly flicking through the pages, a name jumped out almost from the first page. Robert Faulconer, with 'Faulconer' spelt the same way as my wife's maiden name, was the Detroit timber tycoon responsible for setting up Leland & Faulconer, the manufacturing company where the first Cadillacs were made. I then remembered my own Great-Uncle Percy who, having fallen on good times, became the proud owner of one of the earliest of the marque imported into England. I had even seen an old photograph reputed to have been of that almost turn-of-the-century car.

That would be a coincidence, I thought: a five- or ten-times removed tenth or twentieth cousin of my wife's, in America, having helped in the nineteen-nothings to produce a car for my great-uncle, in England; and now, in the nineteen-eighties, here we were messing about with the same make, in England, yet again? Another omen perhaps: fantasy more like. Anyway, regardless of any spurious links with the past, we were fully committed to our course and much time-consuming work lay ahead.

With hindsight, if any of us at that point had had an inkling of what the future held in store, we should have been committed ourselves. Our only saving grace, to this day, was that the glamorous rust-heap depicted on the auctioneer's postcard had eventually changed hands for twice its original estimate: for a staggering one million six hundred thousand pounds – more than two million dollars. There were no second thoughts from any of the team, and the future production target of 'very special Roadsters' rose from half a dozen to fifty. Enthusiasm took on a new meaning: one of instant fame and great riches.

So, as they used to say in that well-known nineteen-sixties South African revue, 'Wait a Minim', which toured London and New York too, "For the sake of the show, let's give it a go"; and we did just that, heading ever deeper into the lion's den.

5. Men At Work

Alan was the first to arrive that Saturday morning to start the dismantling. Mid-forties, medium build, open shirt, loose fitting trousers and sporting a brightly coloured anorak, the highly qualified electrical engineer was quick to explain that his illustrious side-kick would not be accompanying him. There was no need, he said, with the merest hint of disdain, for two of them to be involved with something as *mundane* as a car.

While I expressed some surprise at his assessment of North American motor vehicle electrics, Bruce, pedantic as always and quick to judge, arrived to mediate. Neatly dressed, his norm, but protected by a brand new pair of white overalls, bought especially for the occasion, Bruce was to be in charge of the non-electrics. "When the beer runs out, we run out!" he had said. So the self-professed Back-up had been asked to lay on plenty of nourishment – solid and otherwise.

With the impasse ended and work started, Alan began attaching tags to each electrical item he disconnected, stating what it was and from where it had come, after which he removed each of the looms themselves. Bruce, meanwhile, having taken off the doors, bonnet and trunk lid, bagged up each component in its own individual see-through plastic bag, replacing the relevant fixings either from where they had come or accompanying the relevant object in its bag. I, as the one who supposedly knew all the innermost workings of the Seville, was allowed to direct operations.

As the dismantling progressed, Alan, much to his consternation, found himself confronted with 'wires' that turned out not to be wires. Some were optic fibres for monitoring the head and sidelights, while others proved to be miniature vacuum tubes for the ventilation system and automatic temperature control – and none were prepared to disengage or unplug like normal wires. By the time he had found a 'light' behind the radiator grille that was not a light but the sensor for automatically dipping the headlights, he concluded that, just possibly, there was nothing *mundane* about the electrics in *this* particular car. Reinforcements, therefore, would be joining him the following day.

In time, everything – or almost everything – undid without a major struggle; and nobody damaged anything or themselves, or anyone else for that matter, and our exercise in orderly destruction was soon complete.

The monocoque, that doorless, trunkless metal box, sat un-majestically on part-inflated, grubby whitewall tyres, with the back axle attached at one end and the denuded half-chassis at the other. The component parts were either neatly bagged and hanging round the barn, sitting on one of Frank's flat-bed trailers or, as in the case of the wiring looms, laid out and covered over on sheets of chipboard. There they would all remain, sealed and untouched, until our car-to-be emerged, re-shaped and re-bodied.

Alan, with a final note of realism, fired a parting shot: "If that spider's web of a main wiring loom becomes entangled, forget about trying to unscramble it, tags or no tags."

We duly took note, adding several extra tie-downs to the multitude of plugs and tags that spewed in all directions.

As agreed, we informed Des's right-hand-man that *it* was now ready for collection. Terry, who I suspect found working for Des as much of an entertainment as necessary employment, was true to Des's promise and appeared with a low-loader the following day.

Des, or 'Himself' as he alluded to, operated from a premises that was no more than a larger, cleaner, better fitted out version of the barn. Three individual bays were each approached through their own full-width, full-height roller-shutter doors and all, unlike the barn, had row upon row of modern strip lighting. To the right of these was a dust-filtered, heated spray-booth and paint store and above, up some tight stairs, were a small canteen and an even smaller office. Behind these, rack upon rack of body and trim parts and other paraphernalia over-flowed into the passageway.

Our shell was duly relegated to the bay furthest from the office and as much out of sight from everyday customers as possible.

Terry's job now, using a super-accurate multi-position measuring jig, was to establish a set of reference points on the front, back and on the underside. With these, we could then produce the cutting and re-welding drawings for each stage of the intended transformation.

While assisting Terry one afternoon, I caught sight of an elderly member of his workforce, white hair flowing, hammer and chisel to hand and with a look of steely determination, advancing on our denuded shell. Such a sight did not bode well for the shell. He saw me, stopped and turned.

"It's all right young man," he called out over the general din of voices and machinery, "I'm only taking off the tail pipe and silencer that none of you bothered to remove. You aren't thinking of re-using those on your *special* car are you?"

Taken aback, I felt I should find out a little more about this elderly helper's helper before he took it upon himself to remove something that we had not in fact forgotten.

"Who's that?" I asked Terry. "He appears to do what he likes, when he likes, and generally ignores everyone and everything... he just seems to do his own thing."

"Oh that's Des's Dad," replied Terry. Then, as a supposedly rational explanation: "Des always leaves him here as a sort of substi-tute when he's away."

That explained him to a tee: an older version of Himself – Himself Senior: same attitude, same style – just matured with time.

We got on fine after that. No sooner had he finished removing the exhaust system than I managed to talk him into taking off the back axle and springs, and later even persuaded him to unbolt and remove the front half-chassis. When done, HLN 827V had properly returned to the component bits from which it had originally been made.

Then, one afternoon, with no warning, I arrived to find Des

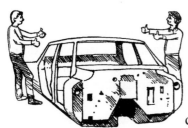

strutting about the body shop as though he had only been away for the weekend. I headed purposefully towards him.

"There it is," I said, pointing with pride to our pathetic shell, "It's completely stripped out, down to the bare metal... just as you wanted. And we already have the first set of cutting plans for you."

"Good. When can you start then?" he asked.

"What do you mean, when can *I* start?" I replied.

Suspecting what he might be suggesting, I launched forth: "The car's dismantled and the plans are done. It's over to *you* now."

"I'm going to need one of you here all the time," he retorted, with a certain dogged determination.

"What do you mean?" I replied, more on the attack and desperately wishing that Jack or Bruce were around for support. "We've finished our bit. You were the one who said you could do the job, and that's why the car is here." Then, as an afterthought: "We can hardly sit around and hold your hand, you know! And, anyway, you would most probably throw us out after an hour or two... one of us would be bound to irritate you."

"Well, how long *can* you spend?" he asked, slightly less dogmatically, realising that I was just as determined.

"About an hour or two, I should think!" was my impulsive reply; after which, on a more conciliatory note: "I suppose one of us could help you get going with each stage... but it'll have to be first thing in the morning or last thing in the afternoon. Anyway, once you get properly stuck in, I'm sure you won't want any of us around then."

"It's not all going to be plain sailing," he replied, "This is very complex and it's got to be done properly... everything has to be accurate, you know."

"Yes, but you're doing it all the time," I said, pointing to the array of vehicles littering the body shop in their various stages of dissection, "If all those aren't *accurate* when you've finished them, you wouldn't have your AA or RAC quality reputation, now would you?"

"Maybe not, but normally we put the cars back the way they started," he replied. "That's not exactly what you want me to do with this one, is it?"

He was right of course: we were not merely changing the odd panel here and the occasional strut there. We were moving vast chunks of metal around like some giant, three-dimensional jigsaw, while at the same time making sure everything ended up according to our none-too-high-tech plans. As I realised the trap into which I had fallen, I also realised there was no going back now: we had effectively destroyed our investment and were heading, ever deeper, into the unknown.

So, never having thought I would be welcome even as a bystander, let alone as a helper, I now appeared to be taking on the role of 'consulting structo-engineer'. With due concern, I double-checked the plans and joined Des for that promised hour or two.

First off, was the removal of the two large protrusions on either side of the forward bulkhead. The one on the right accommodated the ventilation fan and that on the left merely seemed to match up. They would in no way fit within the confines of a thirties-style car and the fan would eventually have to be moved inwards and upwards to fit under the narrower but higher old-style bonnet. Once removed, Des covered each side with a heavy-gauge plate to act as the upper anchor points for the forward space-frames, the other anchor points being the forward ends of the doorsills and each side of the base of the drive-line tunnel.

Next, he started on the centre door pillars. These not only contained the hinges and wiring outlets for the original rear doors – which would now be used as forward-opening fronts – but also the main seat-belt fixings.

Without warning, a string of expletives rang out across the floor, followed by: "How am I supposed to remember which pillar is which? Which one is the *near* side and which is the *off* side... which pillar do I mark *N/S* and which *O/S*?" ending with: "The steering wheel of this thing is on wrong side."

I had long since heard of this terminology for denoting the two sides of a car but had never really understood which referred to which. Anyway, as everything else in life was generally expressed in terms of right and left, I had always done the same with cars.

"Why not mark them 'right-hand' and 'left-hand'... R/H and L/H," I suggested.

"I can't do that," he retorted, "It's not correct."

I remained silent. What was he saying? Was he about to have an argument over some simple terminology like a dedicated mariner would over port and starboard?

"We're trying to build a car," I said. "Surely we can use common, universally understood terms to denote where the various bits come from?"

"It's not right... it ought to be done properly. We're not in Africa or America now, you know."

Such reasoning did not bode well. I had visions of re-marking everything with some surreptitious code. I was about to say something I might have regretted, when I saw Terry move the pillars out of Des's line of view and add a small R/H to one and L/H to the other. An early confrontation was thus avoided.

Now, to prevent any untoward deforming of the remaining structure, he tack-welded bars from various points on the floor onto the bulkhead and onto the rear mudguards. As an added check, and to ensure everything remained within the agreed two-millimetre tolerance, he reattached the multi-position jig.

Why two millimetres, I had asked? Quite simply, because Himself had said this would be so; and who were we to argue with Himself. Personally, having seen the size of some of the shims used in the Seville's make-up, I would have thought he was being a trifle finicky. Indeed, Des was already becoming more than a little possessive about *his* car. Still, at least he was being thorough.

Over the next week or two, as the cutting-up continued, Himself put on a show worthy of the best. As he wrestled with this and struggled with that, cursing and mumbling as he went, his antics and frustration reminded me of when my father and the farm mechanic had attempted to extricate the Ford from the ford. Des would hammer at a bit of the metalwork, drill out some spot-welds and, after a string of instructions to Terry, invariably remove the offending piece with a crowbar.

He did a particularly unceremonious hacksaw job on the front and rear pillars in order to remove the roof. After that he disengaged the forward bulkhead, that complex three-dimensional separator-of-engine-and-cab, partly with a hacksaw and partly by drilling out the spot-welds. When done, Terry was instructed to remove the unwieldy mass to the other side of the workshop.

"Why's this thing so heavy?" Terry complained, as he struggled across the concrete floor?"

"It's good exercise, lad," Des shouted to his thirty-something number two. "Anyway, the heavier it is, the thicker the metal... and all the better for cutting and welding," adding as an afterthought, "Aren't you lucky to be involved!"

Terry declined to answer.

We had long since been warned that if the bulkhead distorted while being dissected and re-welded, the new structure would not comply with the two-millimetre tolerance; and, as far as Des was concerned, without that, there would be no Roadster. Therefore, the thicker metal would not only help each half of the bulkhead hold its shape when the piece down the centre was removed, but the two halves would be easier to weld back together. The metal would not simply "burn up", as he put it.

We now set about marking the piece to be removed: on the dashboard side, on the engine side, at the top, and at the bottom. When done, I left. Apart from Des becoming noticeably fidgety, he was likely to blame me if anything went wrong. For all his awkwardness, though, I was beginning to have firm faith in the one-time customiser of Minis. All the same, with his often bullish, pushy attitude, I was not about to let on.

When I arrived the next day, there, holding pride of place in the middle of the body-shop, were the two halves of the bulkhead with the centre removed; and neither looked as though it was about to disintegrate or fall apart.

"Look," said a jubilant Des, pointing to the dissected complexity, "I did it."

"Yes, that's brilliant Des, that's very clever," I said, realising that our first major hurdle had been successfully completed.

Now, the two effectively narrowed halves had to be re-joined. While doing so, Des needed to re-fit them further back onto what remained of the structure. To add to the intricacy of the operation, he had to position the two halves at a slightly different height and angle than before. Also, due to the inaccessibility of the inside of the bulkhead and the underside of the doorsills, he was unable to use the spot-welder. This, with its great metal-melting pincers, is any body-shop's normal panel-joining gear. Des would therefore have to weld everything with a wire-feed MIG-welder instead: a laborious process that, although generally stronger, creates much more heat, which in turn exacerbates the possibility of distortion.

After tacking on more of his temporary safety bars to help stabilise the structure, Des put the three-dimensional jig back in place as an added check.

While suitably entertaining for the onlookers, it was no fun for the worker. Hour after hour Des battled on, sparks from the welding-gear puncturing his part-bare arms and singeing his half-protected hair, while the fumes from the burning metalwork attacked the innermost depths of his vocal chords; and, the more they did so, the more, in direct proportion, did his vociferous cursing increase. In truth, he would have been better off in Hell's Angels' leather and a World War II gas mask but, being Des, his sole means of defence were the half-open overalls and a hand-held welder's shield.

Once started, no requests from employees or customers alike would detract him from his goal. He welded from side to side, from corner to corner, upside down and right side up, while all the time bending this and prising that until whatever he was working on met up as it should. At times, he would clamber out to check the jig or, after some weld or other had exploded, to adjust a dial; or merely give the welding-gear a good kick. When finished, everything was checked, and then double-checked.

Eventually, as much to Des's surprise as to that of the spectators, all the readings on the jig were within his two-millimetre tolerance. Des looked up, beaming from ear to ear. Yes, a satisfying moment to be sure: a major hurdle had been cleared. That evening, Des, the ever-patient Terry and I retired to the pub for some well-earned drinks.

When next I visited, there, again holding pride of place in the centre of the floor, was a veritable little tub. Formally having been covered in dull reddish-brown primer, the front was now shining jet-black with freshly applied paint and the weld down the centre was quite impossible to see.

"That's very smart, Des," I said. "You can't see where you've joined it... amazing." Then, as I looked more closely, I realised something was amiss. Where were all the fixing bolts and screws that had been left in their correct positions on the front of the bulkhead, especially the three unusual ones for attaching the windscreen wiper motor?

"Where are all the fixings at the front?" I asked, pointing at the bulkhead.

"What fixings?" Des enquired.

"Well, for a start, the irreplaceable windscreen-wiper motor bolts... to say nothing of all the other bolts and screws needed for re-attaching the various components."

I was sure the windscreen-wiper bolts were not irreplaceable, but Bob and his team in Ohio could do without sourcing some ten- and twenty-cent specials for their eccentric friends in England.

"I don't know. They were probably in the way when I was cleaning up," he answered, then added jubilantly, "Look, you can't see the join... it's just as though it was always like this."

"Des," I said, rather more firmly, "it's very smart, but where are all the bolts and screws that you've removed?"

"Oh, I chucked them somewhere in the trunk," he replied, again adding: "Doesn't it look nice?"

"Yes, Des, the bulkhead is very nice but no one's ever going to see it. It's going to be under the bonnet and covered up with all the bits and pieces we will be putting back on again."

"Well *I* can see it, and everyone coming in here now can see it. So it's got to look right," he retorted.

"Good grief, if you're going to personally polish and decorate every weld," I said, clambering into the trunk looking for the bolts and screws, "we won't get this project finished before the turn of the century!"

"That's right, you give it to him, 'Ya'," shouted Terry from across the body-shop, who had long since taken it upon himself to use this vaguely foreign alternative for 'yes' that I tended to use – due mainly, I assume, to its excessive use by the Dutch in Africa.

I eventually found the wiper-motor bolts, along with some of the screws, and returned them to where they belonged. I then noticed that a number of irreplaceable brackets were also missing. They could only have been deliberately removed by un-spotwelding them.

"What's happened to the brackets?" I asked pointing to the top of his shining black metalwork.

"They didn't look right, so I took them off," Des replied, adding, "You can sort all that out later."

I was incredulous.

"But where are they?" I asked

"Oh I think I chucked them in the pit."

"What pit?"

"The one under the car."

I was speechless. I borrowed some overalls and boots and, with the help of an amused Terry, eventually, after much rummaging through much junk, we found the missing brackets.

Himself was a menace. I now understood what he meant by, "Bits'll get broken and bits'll get lost". He may have been very good at what he did but, from now on, I would have to watch every bolt, screw and bracket. Also, I needed to square things; I needed to get my own back on this bossy, over-independent individual.

By chance, several weeks later, some friends of ours were over from Australia. I knew they were both interested in cars and that he was particularly interested in structural engineering. I warned Des that they would be down to see what we were up to.

"This is Jude and Phil from Australia," I said, when we arrived.

After a quick inspection of the bulkhead, I wandered off to check something on the half-chassis propped up against a side wall. While I did so, the conversation apparently veered onto me.

"He's very difficult you know," said Des, "always worrying about his bolts and screws and always thinks he knows best," then, after a pause, he casually asked Phil: "How long have you known him?"

"Oh, five or six years," Phil replied with a smile, indicating that he was speaking for Jude as well.

"And you?" Des enquired, looking at the third person who had accompanied us.

"Oh, about twenty I think," she said.

Des looked at the three of them, then at each, one at a time. "What do you mean *about twenty*?" he asked, in a slow drawn-out voice. There was no reply.

Then, suddenly, somewhat shocked: "You're his wife, aren't you... and I've been saying all those things about him!"

"Don't worry," she quipped without hesitation, "I entirely agree with all you said."

Des never forgot the incident and has never quite forgiven me for not introducing him in the first place. I thought I already had on an earlier occasion. Still, the episode went some way to making up for those missing bolts and brackets: the score had at least been evened just a little.

He did realise in the end the sense of putting back as many components as possible from where they had come. He also realised, with some prompting from the ever-ebullient Sandy, the need for an overall sandblast and repaint once all the welding was complete. A touch of primer between modifications to prevent rust was one thing but all this elaborate painting, often being destroyed by subsequent welding, was a complete waste of time.

Sandy had been down a couple of times to check on the fixing points for the space-frames. With his expertise in vehicle structures, any concern over their soundness had quickly been remedied with some extra reinforcing. "Better safe than sorry," he had gushed with his usual grin and chuckle. Jack too had been in a couple of times, agreeing and, much to our surprise, almost enthusing over everything. At times like these, as the self-styled 'consulting structo-engineer', I merely stood back and observed.

The body critics, the sometimes scaled-down carmaker Bruce and farmer Frank, had each only dropped in once. Bruce, within minutes, had made some pedantic remark – what it was, we never discovered –

resulting in a fierce reaction from Des. Bruce left shortly afterwards and declined to return. Frank had taken one look at what we had so far done and made clear his intention to reserve judgement until later. We ignored what we described as his "lack of imagination" and continued on our course. Frank, too, declined to return.

To give Frank his due, we had come to a point where there was very little similarity to a car, or to any form of motorised transport for that matter, and there was certainly no hint of a likeness to our Roadster. Anyway, what little resemblance there might have been was totally destroyed when Des removed the outer back wings and the rear section of the trunk.

He continued his destructive transformation by rounding off the rear end in line with the Roadster's tail-to-be and adding some crude box-beams as strengtheners. Finally, out of the centre of the beam running sideways across the trunk floor, rose a bracket with an oversize wing-nut: the spare wheel mount.

Seeing that tub steadily take shape, perched majestically on a couple of wooden planks in the furthest corner of Des's body-shop, complete with fitted spare wheel, was both exciting and rewarding. We at last began to feel we were getting somewhere. Sandy, eulogising as always, invariably departed each time with: "Oh, won't she be just fantastic!" while a more cautious Jack tended to end more on the note: "well, it's coming together, isn't it?"

In order to accommodate the original rear doors as forward openers, Des now reinstalled the centre door pillars on the opposite sides in reverse direction from where they had come and finished them off to accommodate the existing roof at its original width and height. This created the more upright, lower look both to the windscreen and to the doors.

Next was the roof itself. While the cutting and re-fixing of the bulkhead might have been the most critical, fitting the roof would be the trickiest. When cut, this normally strong, rigid structure becomes a floppy, potentially useless, piece of semi-formed sheet metal. Worse still, Des had to cut and fold it *twice*. Not only would he have to remove two exact Vs on each side that converged towards the centre, but each of the cut-lines would also have to be minutely arced to account for the roof's barely perceptible sideways curvature.

Himself excelled himself. Having cut along the V-lines with a power hacksaw and folded the roof to the correct angle, he welded the heavy-gauge side-channels to hold the two sections rigid. Then, across the top the roof, he applied small tack-welds every few inches, following up with a damp cloth each time to cool one before doing the next. Finally, with a row of damp cloths down each side to prevent over-heating, he continuous welded from one tack-weld to the next.

After this, he placed the double-folded roof on the centre door pillars with its front end resting on the rather-more-upright wind-screen pillars and its back-end protruding down between the rear mudguards. Again, he put the jig back in place.

As always, he set about the welding as though his life depended on it. No sooner done than he made up and added the forward centre divider for the two-piece flat windscreen. Yet again, everything ended up within his two millimetres. Still, I have no doubt that, if not, he would have undone the lot and tried again; or simply downed tools and demanded another roof.

Anyway, a true little aeroplane cockpit, if ever there was one, was now there for all to see. So elated were we at this, that we decided to leave the doors until later, until after the pair of space-frames had been fitted. Why? Because I think we knew, just as I had discovered at university that, as complex as our space-frame arrangement might be, car doors we considered to be one worse.

Looking back now, we were really only doing what my friend and I had done to that wind-up tin-plate toy car as children. We had disman-tled and subsequently destroyed our toy, again on the pretext of making something better, and now the something better was taking shape – so why spoil the fun.

Added to that, the Christmas to New Year holiday was coming up and our little creation was about to be returned to Frank's barn, to be assessed – and potentially played with – before proceeding to the next stage. All very exciting: but little did we realise that the true challenge was about to start and much of the *fun* was about to run out.

6. *Help!*

"But Jack," I said, "I've moved the engine and transmission backwards and forwards, up and down, within all its possible limits, but there's no way I can get the steering shaft to miss the engine."

Our little cockpit had been returned to Frank's near-freezing barn and was now sitting majestically in the centre of a wide expanse of nothing. The back axle had been re-fitted, the half-chassis was crudely fixed in place, a number of under-bonnet components were attached to the front of the narrowed bulkhead and the engine was hanging up front, clumsily suspended from Jack's crane. To complete the picture, the radiator, supposedly representing the fearsome front of a Roadster-to-be, had been up-ended between the front wheels.

I had already spent a couple of days, partly on my own and partly with Jack, working with this newly assembled amalgam and now, halfway through the Christmas to New Year holiday, what little progress had been made was at a standstill. If only Bruce had not been sent off to Australia by his employers. Despite all his instant answers and pedantic reactions, he might just have been able to throw some light on it all.

"Are you sure the engine is lined up with the centre of the chassis, and that the chassis and the altered structure are also lined up correctly?" Jack enquired with his normal solid reasoning.

"Look, see for yourself," I replied, pointing towards the two metal bars running the length of the doorsills and forward to the front wheels. "We tack-welded these on for reference points and now, as a further check, I've added this," I said, pulling on a wire V, its base point aimed forwards with its two upper ends attached to corresponding matching bolts on each side of the bulkhead. "It's all spot on, but the steering shaft just won't fit."

"How much by?" Jack asked.

"About half an inch." Then, continuing in mounting frustration: "When you, Bruce and I originally checked, before we cut it all up, our calculations proved it would work. Certainly, we always knew this area would be a tight fit but that it would still work. Now the whole thing's a bloody shambles!"

Several other bits were refusing to oblige. The air-conditioning unit on the right of the bulkhead was interfering with the top of the engine, the transmission fouled the left side of the narrowed bulkhead and the radiator was not going to be the minor modification of up-ending and shortening it as hoped.

The complications with the air-conditioning and the radiator could be overcome, but the steering shaft and the tunnel were altogether different. If we had to move the steering column to miss the engine, then we would be unable to use the existing dashboard with all its switches, gauges, air-ducting and everything else. If that happened, one of the main advantages of using a fully engineered, already-tooled structure was fading into oblivion.

"Jack," I said, "a week ago, although we knew things were becoming complicated, we were all so excited about what we had done. Now, here we are, trundling around with a mess of an engine in amongst a collection of cut-up and re-welded metal, starting to look like a bunch of Professor Potts attempting to make Chitty Chitty Bang Bang all over again."

I drew a deep long breath, then continued: "This whole ill-conceived idea is supposed to be the creation of a luxury Roadster as a prototype for more, not some half-baked, roughed-up stock car. Where on earth have we gone wrong?"

He saw my frustration but, being meticulous by nature and normally working in thousandths of an inch, he was wondering no doubt how anyone could have made a mistake by as much as half an inch. As Jack's family was waiting – and as the crisis appeared to be mostly of my doing – he wished me luck and left.

Sandy was the other person who might be able to help. Although keen to be left to enjoy his well-earned festive break, he had not yet seen this latest stage and might like an excuse to do so. He did, arriving as always in short-sleeve shirt and brightly coloured tie neatly tucked into smartly pressed trousers: his standard attire winter or summer.

While I was rapidly falling out of love with the lamentable conglomerate, Sandy, no sooner than in the barn, took entirely the opposite tack. With his infectious smile and bubbling enthusiasm, he immediately expounded all the virtues of the little cockpit on wheels.

"You can see what it's going to be like. The shape will be fantastic, and that aerodynamic flow. Look at the long bonnet and the tiny windscreen... just like an aeroplane on wheels!"

"But the steering goes through the engine," I said caustically, as I tried desperately to visualise his "aerodynamic flow".

"Oh, but you can overcome that," he said, as though Jack and I had barely begun to look for a solution.

"I appreciate your confidence," I replied coldly, "but we can't have your lot making up and attaching the space-frames unless we can sort this out first. The steering wheel does have to connect to the front wheels, you know."

"But it doesn't miss by much," he said, as he looked at the offending shaft spewed sideways protruding through an imaginary up-and-over bonnet.

"A miss is a miss," I said. Then, after a pause: "There's so much being crammed into the new narrower design that we can't alter the position of anything; and the engine and transmission has to line up in the centre as before."

"Anything's possible, anything's possible," he blurted confidently, quite unperturbed at my concern.

In the end, all I could extract from Sandy was his continued passion for the glorious car-to-be. He left, smiling and relaxed, as though nothing was wrong. Still, we all loved his blind faith and, while not being exactly what I was looking for at that moment, it did cheer me up. In the end, his ongoing fervour, along with a certain amount of my bloody-minded obstinacy and a natural dislike of failure, forced me to keep looking for an answer.

The next day, while checking over the other discrepancies, convincing myself that the project should, after all, be scrapped, a thought occurred: a stupid thought maybe but, any possibility, however remote, had to be examined.

What if the engine and transmission had not been mounted in the centre of the car in the first place? That would explain two of the problems in one: the steering shaft and the transmission tunnel. Yet, if the engine were off centre, the whole tunnel and the differential housing on the back axle would have to be off centre too. Either that or the propeller shaft ran at an angle down the length of the car. Both possibilities seemed very unlikely. Furthermore, the difficulty of carrying out such a check on pre-formed, rounded-off metalwork almost prevented me from doing so.

When I did, I re-checked and re-checked again. I stood for a full ten minutes staring at that mess of metal. So it was true: everything, engine, transmission tunnel and back axle, was off centre by just over half an inch. To this day, I still marvel as to why somebody went to such trouble to shift the power train to the right by this seemingly insignificant amount. I am sure there must have been a good reason; but what, I suspect we will never know.

In the end, all I could do was to chuckle at Sandy's prediction of eventually finding an answer – albeit with a certain irritation. I just sat there, staring at that skinless heap with its reference bars and reference wires, and that great filthy lump of an engine hanging in the void up front. One thing was for sure, without more help, especially with Bruce having gone to Australia, we were walking a tightrope: and a foolhardy one at that.

In the longer term, help with some of the more complicated detail would come in the form of Lionel, the qualified auto-engineer recommended by our motor insurers. He was no greenhorn, though, and would likely crucify us had we not at least solved some of the basics before he appeared.

By asking around, we discovered that more immediate help might come in the form of Bill. Bill was a good all-rounder, who spent much of his time working with Morgans – those timeless wood-and-aluminium sports racers that have remained virtually unchanged for as long as anyone can remember. I telephoned him.

Receiving an affirmative to my: "Is that Bill?" I continued with: "You don't know me, but I'm told you might be able to help with a project we've started. It's a bit unusual and I'm afraid it's got somewhat out of hand."

"Oh, what's the project?" he asked, a note of relaxed keenness wafting down the line.

"Well, it's difficult to describe. You see, we've cut up a '78 Seville and, for want of a better description, I suppose you could say we're trying to make a sort-of large Morgan out of it. I think you need to see it... that is if you're interested in being involved."

No doubt the pause that followed was indicative of his trying to decide by what stretch of the imagination anyone could assimilate a large Seville to a diminutive Morgan.

"Yes, I could be interested," he said eventually. Then, after further hesitation, "I've got a couple of projects on at the moment but the racing season doesn't start for a month or two yet."

"Oh, you're into racing are you?" I interjected.

"Yes, but I don't do much myself. I let other people do the damage and then they pay me to repair it. We get the usual things, burned-out engines, stripped gears and a bit of body damage."

"Oh yes?" I replied, a little flatly, as I contemplated the patience he must have. I would go nuts if someone kept wrecking the same things over and again and repeatedly asked me to fix them. The banter ended and we agreed to meet that evening.

Short, mid-forties, slight of build, with dark blue Shetland jersey covering a blue checked shirt over dark tan corduroy trousers, Bill stood silently making a roll-up beside the barn. With cigarette lit, he rubbed his chin and eyed me purposefully through his horn-rim glasses. I had the distinct feeling that he was still mulling over the likely sanity of any cutters up of Sevilles. Having introduced myself, we headed into the barn.

He batted not an eyelid at the scene before him. Whether

confused, or whether the sight of the denuded cockpit appealed to his sense of humour, I had no idea. If nothing else, I think he felt sorry for us. He had now come across people who destroyed cars without the fun of racing them first.

Having pored briefly over the plans: "How much time are you going to be able to spend with me?" he asked. Then, without waiting for an answer: "I've never seen one of these Sevilles close to, but what you've got here has to be one of the most complex bits of motorcar ever made... even before you cut it up." He finishing off with: "By golly, just look at the size and strength of all that metal." He turned, waiting for my answer.

"I'm afraid I can't spend much time, I'm fully committed with what I'm doing already." I paused. Receiving only a fixed stare, I continued: "When we started, I never envisaged anyone wanting me around after the planning stage. Now I'm told there's too much stored up here" – motioning to my head – "and that it would take too long to put it all on paper." After a further pause: "I could, I suppose, spend some time in the evenings, if that would help?"

"Well," he said, "the job's got to be done. I'm prepared to work late afternoons through until ten o'clock most evenings. I won't charge too much, but I'm going to need another pair of hands... and I'm also going to need you, or someone, to direct me on the detail." At which he looked up at the very basic farmyard lighting throwing its muted glow on the darkly painted corrugated iron: "And we're going to need a bit more light." Again after a pause: "How much time can you spend on that basis?"

Here was someone I had only just met saying he was prepared to work evening after evening at a reduced rate, just to get us out of our self-dug hole. I had to agree to something, whether our budget could stand the additional commitment or not.

"How about if I, or one of the others maybe, joined you most days around five o'clock and worked through from there?"

"Fine," he said, "and what about weekends? There's a lot of work to be done before we get anywhere near fitting a body."

"All right," I said, realising that somehow I would eventually be forgiven by the family, "most weekends, but not all."

I was also sure that we could install some extra lighting. The windowless barn was far from ideal for the intricate work that lay ahead, and memories flooded back of overhauling an Aston engine in the greenhouse: no such luck this time.

Surprisingly, despite the trauma, Des's charges had been less than expected. Also, if Bill could finish the majority of the metal work, including making and tacking together the pieces for the space-frames, and not, as originally intended, have Sandy's lot do it all, that would also help keep to budget.

When our evenings together began in earnest, I soon learnt just how patient was the not-too-speedy but eminently thorough Bill. On many an occasion, the 'walking set of mental plans' attached to the 'extra pair of helping hands' were not as efficient as he might have hoped. As often as not, while in brain mode, I managed to get some design detail wrong or, while in helping hands mode, misalign or misplace something.

Yet Bill, roll-up to hand or ever ready tucked behind his ear, never criticised. He merely pointed to the error of the moment and, in relation to the 'brain', would request further information or, in the case of the 'hands', would give fresh instructions. Thankfully, from time to time, Jack came along to lend weight to both brain and hands.

When Bill had completed the pieces for the space-frames, along with the attaching brackets for the centre and forward pairs of chassis mounts – the rear mounts remaining unaltered in order to retain the integrity of the original car – he booked Sandy's foreman for a Saturday morning to stitch it all together. After several hours' welding, alternating from one side to the other to keep any undue heat distortion to a minimum, Bill checked the references.

He looked up, concerned: "The two forward reference points are three millimetres different in height."

"What?" I exclaimed. "*Three* millimetres! Why? How on earth can we cure it?"

I looked at Sandy's foreman.

"Don't look at me," he said. "I'm only doing the welding. Anyway, what's the problem with a three millimetre difference?"

"We're supposed to be working to a maximum of two millimetres," said Bill.

"Are you telling me that this monster of a car, with all its alterations and additions, is being made to a two-millimetre tolerance? You must be kidding," he said.

"But Des says we have to." I said with concern.

"You're out of your minds. You don't need that sort of accuracy on a one-off. You're not using standard body panels or the like. Believe me, I've done enough of this sort of thing to know."

I guess he was right. As some of the chassis shims were well over three millimetres thick, why should it matter if there was a three-millimetre overall difference. We could simply add a shim or two here or there. Still, if Des had got wind of it, I have no doubt he would have ordered the whole thing cut up and re-done.

Yet, if we had worked to a lesser accuracy, some error or other could have compounded itself into a disastrous ten or more millimetres, ending up with a lop-sided body or even a lop-sided car. So, mindful of Des's likely reaction, caution prevailed and we continued with his two millimetres. The three-millimetre variation, still there to this day, was never again mentioned.

With that finished, Bill soldiered on with the numerous alterations and additions, resorting almost daily to producing drawings of one- or two-off brackets to be made up at a local sheet-metal works. We soon discovered that there was not a straight or parallel bit of metal in that entire car. Some giant press had beaten out every piece. Even cross-members that looked like small railway lines had been formed as though they were made from plasticine. Therefore, as nothing was effectively straight, neither could any of the new brackets be straight, and each and every one had to be individually cut and beaten to fit.

Evening after evening, Bill and I carried on like a couple of black-smiths, adding many an extra hour to a steadily elongating project. In time, though, with the assistance of whomever and whenever – Alan even taking a break from his electrical work to help dismantle the front suspension – we reached a double milestone: sandblasting and repainting followed by the inaugural visit of the professional auto-engineer, Lionel.

The sandblasters, four of them in white overalls and matching helmets, arrived as though straight from outer space. Bill, tobacco pouch and roll-ups ever to hand, and one of Sandy's willing helpers spent most of the day moving items between the blasting outside the barn and the painting inside, being sure that never the two should meet. Des would not appreciate a rough sandpaper finish to his sweated two-millimetre toil. I, of necessity, had been instructed to "keep watch". To have ended up with some of the smaller pieces, precariously strung along a bar on a couple of axle stands, discharged into the new crop of wheat surrounding the barn would not help the project's timely completion.

When done, and with nothing lost, we manhandled everything into a seemingly orderly state and set about tidying up the barn. With Lionel's visit imminent, and needing all the credibility we could muster, the ebullient Sandy was coerced into joining us on the day. Bill's practical knowledge together with my general engineering would count for something but Sandy's expertise and structural engineering qualifications along with his infectious devotion to the cause should, we hoped, count for more.

When Lionel arrived, we all three greeted him as one. At which, after the normal pleasantries, we ushered him into the barn. Heavy spectacled, stern, but intermittently sparkling, he began making short sucking noises, interspersed with: "Yes, yes, I see... yes, yes, I see".

Apart from the inadequate lighting rendering the blackened pieces almost indistinguishable from their surroundings, I doubt he could *see* at all. Helpfully, or so we thought, we had spread the pieces about the barn so that our new team member could better experience every-thing.

"And what are these for?" he asked, as he looked questioningly at the matching struts angled downwards and inwards at the front of each of the space-frames.

"They're for attaching the forward pair of chassis mountings," said Bill, as he pointed to the bottom of the half-chassis leaning up against the wall with the point of our newly-made A-frame attached at the other end finishing up in the eaves.

The more I watched, the more I realised that he was as confused as everyone else when first setting eyes on it all. In truth, as a highly respected engineer, to be thrown headlong into this profusion of unorthodox mechanics, and in the middle of someone's farmyard, was a bit much. The more he looked, the more I realised that, without the plans, he had little idea of what we were up to.

When eventually he saw the plans and accompanying calculations, and understood how and why everything was supposed to fit, the change was immediate. He became inspired and animated, strutting back and forth asking any number of questions, while all the time making detailed notes and sketches. All of a sudden, he disappeared outside to return shortly clutching a camera. He then proceeded to photograph every piece, one at a time, and all together.

"What do you think?" Sandy asked with a broad grin, when the clicking had died down. "What should or shouldn't we have done differently?"

"Well, what you've done all makes sense," Lionel replied. "It's just so unusual. You wanted to create the structural rigidity, while at the same time retain the ride qualities... and, personally, I can't see a better way."

We were delighted. Here was the expert, who also represented our insurers, telling us that we had done nothing unwise or stupid; or at least not in engineering terms. As for the wisdom of having started the project: on that, he made no comment.

"You've got to criticise what we've done in some way or other," I said, noting Sandy's smiling agreement and Bill's imperceptible nod.

"Well," he said, a little hesitant, "I must confess I've been looking at the size and thickness of the steel members of your space-frame set-up. I would have thought they were a little over-designed... they're like giant battering rams!"

We all laughed and, after Lionel had made some helpful suggestions and a tentative date for his next visit, we went our separate ways. Fortunately, the over-designed battering rams, as Lionel called them, would, if nothing else, help to ballast a much-lightened front of a much-modified car.

Within days, we had reassembled both the front and rear suspension and the half-chassis too, and bolted them all back onto the now named 'hulk'. We fitted a mock-up radiator cowl, made up by the sheet-metal works as a pattern, and stood back. One look at the assembled structure and, without reservation, we convinced ourselves that we were home and dry. Just a case of making the doors and a few other bits and pieces, sending the structure to the coachbuilders for a body, putting everything back inside, then finishing off with a coat of paint. As optimists, that was surely one of our finest hours.

Still, the recurring belief that we were always further ahead than we really were, was probably the single greatest motivator throughout the entire project: a sort-of ongoing "where ignorance is bliss, 'tis folly to be wise". In fact, so ecstatic were we at this point, both with Lionel's praise as well as with the sudden transformation to a semblance of a car, that somewhat unwisely we informed all and sundry of the project's existence.

First on the scene were the teenage friends of our teenage daughter. They arrived in their droves, their eagerness knowing no bounds. Like us marauding teenagers back in Africa in the fifties and sixties, they produced no end of ideas, even suggesting the car be put on the road there and then. "It would make a great stock car... really cool!" one of them was heard to mutter. Such a remark was not intended for our ears; or so we liked to believe.

The misguided admission also produced numerous suggestions from well-wishing friends and friends of friends too. There were any number of awkward questions: to some, we had answers and, to others, our response was weak and unconvincing. In truth, the state of the engineless hulk, with its part-made doors and steadily rusting mock-up radiator cowl, was not the most inspiring sight to anyone remotely used to normal, one-piece motorcars.

Then, to my consternation but also partly to my satisfaction, Bill proceeded to prove that car doors are a complexity that should never have been invented. My idea at university had perhaps not been so hare-brained after all. Even the Duke Boys, in 'The Dukes of Hazard' television series, had come to a similar conclusion: just climb in and out through the windows.

Apart from the difficulty with the locking mechanisms, with their multitude of rods and levers, all of which needed to be altered and re-connected, Bill also had to create the sweeping curve to the new front edges of the doors. To achieve this, he had to cut out, then painstakingly weld along their entire lengths, five individual concentric steps, starting from the inside trim-face and ending with the door-skin fixing on the outside. None of us could see any other way of matching up to the original pressed-out strength.

The ever-patient Bill then set about reinstalling the massive side-impact protectors to each door. We could have easily done without these but Lionel's reassurances, instead of tempting us to be more flexible in our approach, had only encouraged us to finish everything off in true battleship style.

With the doors done, Bill started on the windscreen wipers, just one of many other tasks still to do. He began by mounting the spindles for the wiper arms just below the front of the new windscreen, then connected the spindles to the motor down inside the bulkhead by shortening the linkages. So simple was this that Bill and I felt a full-blown test to be superfluous, especially as activating the wiper-motor without the full wiring harness was no easy task. Yet, as Jack pointed out, caution prevailing, any attempt to cure a design fault inside the top of the old bulkhead, especially after the new aluminium body had been fitted, would be a near impossibility.

So, out came the wiring diagrams and Alan made up a suitable miniature set of cables with all the necessary connections. Then, with everything connected and complete with brand new miniature wiper blades, the test commenced: just to be sure.

Just to be sure? That was a joke. None of us could have foreseen that two pitiful waving arms destined to clean a couple of diminutive pieces of flat glass would be quite so mind-blowing. To our disbelief, the driver's blade started off backwards, changed direction with a jerk, slowed down over the centre, accelerated again and, catching the bottom of the surround, bent itself in the middle. While all this was happening, its mate on the passenger's side moved through such a small arc that the passenger would have been hard pushed to see anything at all.

Recounting this to a friend shortly afterwards, he disdainfully replied: "Oh, didn't you know there are design companies that specialise in windscreen-wiper actuation? It's very complex, you know, and it's all done by computers now."

No, we did not know such things, nor did we wish to be enlightened as to just how blinkered was our approach; any more than we wished to know that computers – at a time well prior to their being even remotely user-friendly – could be of any assistance whatsoever. In fact, due almost entirely to those wipers, together with that other question-able task of fitting the original motorbike-like front mudguards into the front of the space-frames, we found time was fast running short for the agreed July deadline.

When the newly-made cowl and headlight bar, welded together by 'eyes in his fingers', were firmly in place and all the other structural work complete, a now familiar statement was to be heard: "It's really beginning to look like a car!" Oh yes, some car, some imagination.

In fact, in order to help catch up, we were about to have a birthday party in the barn – mine. This would be our son's first re-introduction to HLN 827V since being taken for a ride that first day. What would a car-loving six-year-old think: all the excitement of Dad making a special car?

When the time came, he walked into the barn, stared blankly at all before him, and turned, wide-eyed and in obvious disbelief, to pronounce: "Dad! What have you done to the car?"

No remark could better have demonstrated how blind we were to the realities of what we were doing and, unfortunately for me, the statement will live on in the family indefinitely.

Lionel arrived a few days later to cast his auto-engineering eyes over what we had been up to and to make sure that no "stupidities", as he put it, were about to be covered up by the new body. On entering the barn, he stopped, looked, almost as though in a trance, then slowly strode towards the newly embellished and near fully-assembled structure. Very quietly but very thoroughly, he examined every nut, bolt and weld that had been added since his last visit. Then, with another photographic session over, he launched forth.

"You are *obsessed* with over-designing, aren't you," at which he added with a chuckle: "There's very little chance of anything coming adrift on this lot... even if rammed by a bus!"

Just as on his first visit, we finished with a laugh, happy to have played safe with over rather than under design. As he left, Bill and I had the feeling that, although more positive, Lionel still seemed unconvinced; just as farmer Frank, our landlord, seemed to have long since become so too. Yet worrying about their belief or disbelief would be of little help. All we could do was battle on.

Finally, there were the bodybuilders' plans and templates still to be done. "How," someone had asked, "are you going to be sure to create accurate three-dimensional reality from your tenth scale two-dimensional drawings?"

"Why not have the plans photographed and blown up to full size," suggested the owner of a local print works. "Modern black & white photographic paper is very stable. It doesn't alter with changes in temperature and humidity like when I was a lad. Back then, if you had used it, you'd for sure have ended up with one side of your car different to the other!"

We noted the seriousness of the light-heartedness and dispatched the plans to a graphics house to be photographed and enlarged – to within Des's two millimetres of course.

We worked on, night after night, ignoring the strains and discomforts; but always well stocked with a surfeit of sustenance, as supplied by the ever-tolerant Back-up. Then, suddenly, late one evening in mid-July, the task at hand was finished. We sat back, Bill, Jack and I, in those trusty deck chairs, almost a year after having first entered the barn with HLN 827V, and raised several cans of beer to our current success. Next morning, perched high up on Bill's trailer, with cowl and headlamps gleaming up front and the spare wheel proudly mounted in the void behind, the blackened structure was on its way.

The very next day, we set off, a family freed from an overbearing extra-curricular project, on a long overdue summer holiday, safe in the knowledge that the budding Roadster was someone else's headache for a change.

7. Unwelcome Hurdle

"What do you mean, you don't think you can do the job?" I said in disbelief.

Arriving at the coachbuilders, I had been informed by the owner that *if* they were able to make the body for the Roadster, which was a big 'if', the task would take considerably longer than estimated and would cost more. Yet in the same breath, he was saying they had found a subcontractor to make the wings. Why, I thought, if he was saying they were unlikely to be able do the job, was he talking of subcontracting some of it out? Also, if they were unable to do the job, how could it take longer or cost more? Was I missing something?

"You see," he continued, with a note of reverence, "we lost our foreman... the elderly gentleman who came with me on my visit to you earlier in the year."

"Oh," I said, concerned. "I am sorry. How did it happen? Was it sudden?"

"It was about three months ago," he replied, a little more casually. "He had to go, he was too slow." Then, as though nothing was amiss: "But we've got a very good new young man started."

Was I hearing correctly? We had delivered the car to this company for a particular craftsman to construct a body using techniques and costings determined and agreed by him and the owner and, now, several weeks later, I was being told that the man had neither fallen ill nor died but had had his employment arbitrarily terminated for his apparent ongoing slowness.

"Why, may I ask, didn't you inform us of this earlier?"

A silence reminiscent of a distant, windless Scottish moor was followed by renewed confidence: "Come and meet and have a chat with our new young expert. He'll explain everything, he'll sort it all out, you'll see."

In an outer office, sitting amongst a clutter of papers, which included the Roadster's none-too-high-tech plans, was a lad in his late twenties deep in conversation with the quickly-introduced works manager, whom I had not previously met. As our now four-way conversation progressed, regardless of my prompting, they all evaded the one all-important issue: our denuded black hulk needed a pretty body at a sensible price: and sooner rather than later.

"Why don't we continue this around the car," I suggested, partly in hope that something constructive might come of it, and partly in growing irritation. "At least then we can evaluate each problem, one at a time, and relate each to the plans."

As we entered the workshop, there, stretched before us, with barely a spare square inch between them, was an assortment of four-wheeled icons, ranging from the thirties through to the late sixties. One notable exception, forlorn and alone, tucked not too neatly into a lean-to alcove, was our blackened hulk. As we headed in its direction, still on the move, I was introduced to an even younger young man, whom I was casually informed was the 'wing maker'. Almost at the same time, and for no apparent reason, I suddenly received a diatribe from the coachbuilders' new young man on the theories of computer-aided body design.

There were those computers again, always needed to design things: first windscreen wiper actuation, now entire bodies. He rambled on, quite unworried that there had been no computers around when our body style had first appeared. Why, I thought, did I have to listen to all this? Why also, having just completed the major part of the project, was I hearing little voices from within saying, yet again, that we had possibly only just begun?

What finally prompted me to say what I did, I have no idea, but say it I did, all the same.

"Firstly," I declared, staring the owner in the face, "if you weren't such a nice little man, and it wasn't such a lovely summer's day," then pointing to some newly cut grass outside: "I would take you out onto that beautifully mown lawn… and I would thump you."

There was complete silence; so I continued.

"Secondly," I said, while banging the edge of my hand on my forehead, "I have had this whole project up to here and I am going to take this great lump of metal and put it in the nearest crusher... and that'll be an end to it."

At which, the works manager led the new young man slowly away, the owner developed an inane grin reminiscent of Stan, of Laurel and Hardy fame, while the wing maker, smartly dressed in dapper attire, moved not a muscle. Still nobody spoke, so I continued once more.

"What have I, and all the others, done to deserve this? How on earth could we ever have been so stupid to believe that a modification project like this could ever have succeeded... especially with you lot involved?"

With which, and with the ongoing silence, I turned and walked out into the sunlight and onto the neatly cut lawn. At least I could enjoy both of those. Instinctively, I looked up to see that no impending clouds would darken that too.

I walked along, contemplating the fate of the blackened hulk. With no available coachbuilder there would be no pretty body; and with no pretty body, there was no car. It was now abundantly clear that we should never have started the project. Abandoning it was the only answer: even at this late stage.

The extra expenditure since the cut-off date had been minimal. I would just have to live with the fact that I had overseen a disaster. Disappointing for everyone involved, yes, but I could not propose at this late stage throwing more good company money after bad.

As I walked across the lawn, I sensed someone following: I stopped and turned. There was the wing-maker, the younger young man, a veritable teenager in fact. Strong-faced with an ever-so-slightly cheeky look, he was obviously trying to understand who and what he was dealing with. As it later turned out, Gavin the wing maker was all of twenty years old.

"I don't know if I should interfere," he started, "but it would be a terrible shame to put that car into a crusher." He paused for reaction. Getting none, he went on: "I do believe, that with help from you and whoever else has been working with you, I could make the aluminium body, the whole thing, not just the wings."

"How?" I asked, barely believing my ears. "You heard what they said. How can you do what they can't? And what could *we* do to help with the bodywork? None of us are even in the motor industry, let alone in this specialist field."

"They told me in there that you and some others have completely designed and made that structure. From what I've seen, if you've been able to do that, then I can show you how to do the next stage." He hesitated, obviously trying to gauge my thoughts, then continued: "That car should be bodied using tubular steel framework, not with wood as they suggest."

What a day: the youngest amongst us appeared to be the sanest. Tubular steel, not wood: just as Bill and I had first thought. No, there would be too many unforeseen problems: what he was suggesting could never work. Yet, here was a young man with enough faith in what we had done to approach someone who, for all he knew, spent his time threatening to *flatten* people. He was also suggesting that Bill and I and the others could, without any previous experience, venture into the realms of specialist coachbuilding.

Was he mad, or was this some huge compliment? Lionel, that super-professional auto-engineer, had said we had done some impressive structural work so far. Perhaps there was truth in what this apparent teenager was saying after all. Surely, though, there was no possibility of us making all of the body structure ourselves?

"Even if, with your help," I said, "we were able to fabricate most of the structure, what makes you think you could handle *all* the panelling? What if you encounter problems partway through? Then we will have thrown even more money down the drain."

"That won't happen," he replied, with a conviction that was undoubtedly born out of his belief.

Even then, he still might not be able to talk us through our part. No, at his age, he was bound to come up against all kinds of problems, any one of which could prove insurmountable.

Quite unmoved by my negatives, he threw down a challenge: "Would you at least be prepared to visit my premises and inspect some of my work... and then maybe discuss it further before making a final decision?"

I looked him hard in the eye and realised I had no option: "All right," I said, "that's the least we can do."

A week later, after the never-tiring Bill had made the long round trip to return our semblance of a car to Frank's barn, I arrived at Gavin's works. Gavin, together with an even younger helper, worked in a small neat and tidy establishment tucked away along a side-road in Berkshire. The complex of converted semi-industrial units, better suited to a previous age, sported a mixture of brick, wood and iron buildings linked together with paved concrete roadways. It was a veritable maze, all of which produced an immediate sense of being lost as soon as entering.

Gavin, wiry, slight of build, always seemed to sport just a hint of a wry, dry smile. More often than not, this would progress to a cheeky semi-sideways look. The dapper attire, when first we met, had appropriately changed to clean, white, well-pressed overalls.

As he went through the range of his work, some in photographs and some to hand, the half-smile and cheeky look remained. If this was all genuinely of his own doing, Gavin was undoubtedly capable of some very complex work.

"Where did you learn all this?" I asked. "I don't see how you could have gained such experience at your age."

A ruffled frown settled across his brow: "I've been working on panelling since I was ten years old."

"What do you mean?" I exclaimed, then added facetiously: "They don't operate child labour around here, do they?"

After a pause and semi-sideways look: "Well, my father is in the trade, and my grandfather was too. When my father was younger, he was involved in some special work for Rolls-Royce," at which he added, almost as an afterthought but with obvious pride, "and my grandfather made engine cowlings and nose cones for Lancaster bombers during World War II."

"Good grief," I said, "that explains it. It's in the blood." Then added, for no particular reason really: "Most of the farmers in East Anglia are farmers' sons... they can literally *smell* the weather!"

Without waiting for, or noting any reactions to my irrelevancies, we set about attempting to rescue a potentially redundant blackened hulk. A glimmer of hope was appearing after all.

Conveniently, for teacher and newfound student alike, Gavin had a tubular framed car in a nearby shed with its panelling removed. He explained the dos and don'ts of these body structures, where to fix this and where to weld that, and generally how to tie the framework together in order properly to support the panelling. No sooner was this initial lesson complete, than he calmly announced that he would talk us through the rest on the telephone. His enthusiasm, without doubt, was very infectious; but I was far from convinced by such optimistic reasoning.

Then, having given an idea of how long and what might be the cost, he proposed we commission some bucks for the wings. I thought he was being funny and made some silly remark about the four-legged kind in Africa. I was quickly put in my place and informed that, in the coachbuilding trade, a buck is a dismantlable, reversible jig rather like a three-dimensional slotted toy. He explained how it acted as an open wooden skeleton around which the eventual self-supporting wing is shaped. One for the front wings and one for the rear wings would ensure accurate mirror image creations on each side.

After everything we had been through, and especially with the other lot of coachbuilders, I was sure that we could well do without a lop-sided car. If we did continue, I had no doubt that we would agree to his request.

I returned home and, later that day, contacted Jack and Bill to see what they thought, genuinely and unemotionally. Also, could Bill even continue: the whole affair had been far more time-consuming than any of us had envisaged and I would quite understand if he wanted out. There were indications too that prices in the classic car market were beginning to drop. Still, even if prices halved, the Mercedes 540K having sold for double its original estimate, we would only be back where we started.

"Well?" I asked, looking at them both.

As so often with Jack and Bill, there was silence: only this time a little more protracted than usual. Neither of them were super-keen twenty-somethings who thought, single-handedly, they could conquer all about them: both had seen many a scheme come to nothing or flounder half way through.

Bill, fumbling with a roll-up, was first: "If this 'young Gavin' you talk of is so sure that we are capable of completing the structure, and you are happy that he really is able to do the aluminium panelling, then we had better just get on and do it!"

Jack, after the usual steady protracted thought, gave his: "I'll go along with that" then, after a further pause, "and I'll also try to get down to the barn some evenings and lend a hand."

Good old philosophical Bill, even with the motor racing season in full swing, he still somehow felt unable to let the project down. Deep down he was hooked, as was Jack too. Somehow, regardless of any apparently insurmountable obstacles, a blind faith seemed to be coming to the fore. How the Back-up would react to this latest development, about which I had so far said little, was something else. I would somehow have to convince her of the wisdom of our ways without ending up on the receiving end of the proverbial rolling pin.

Although Gavin was delighted with the go-ahead, I was still not so sure. To be investing in an expensive aluminium body with the only professional involved, apart from Lionel, barely out of his teens had to be madness in the extreme. I could only hope that I would not regret such a potentially foolhardy decision and, with that in mind, the three of us, Jack Bill and I, decided to keep some of the more questionable detail from the others.

Bill and I, with Jack's very welcome assistance and occasionally that of the ever-helpful normally electrically-minded Alan, now settled back to working evenings and weekends in that familiar old barn. Being summer, we could throw open those giant rusty steel doors and enjoy the flowing golden corn on the rolling hills, interrupted only by the occasional far-off farm building or church steeple.

The change from wood to metal for the body-formers required a number of rethinks. The back end would have to be made up with a criss-cross of bent-to-shape steel tubes welded onto the structure and the same would apply around the bulkhead in front of the cab. The doors, like any modern car door, would simply be skinned, metal-to-metal; and the sides of the body were flat and therefore would present no problems.

That was short-lived. During one of young Gavin's telephone directives, we were informed that no panels on any original thirties car were straight. Every curve was compound: those difficult-to-make three-dimensional curves that we had deliberately decided not to use on our ill-conceived project at university. There were only two exceptions: the sides of the bonnet, although complicated by ventilation louvres, were perfectly flat and the two bonnet tops were simply rolled along their length, and therefore non-compound.

"Well, you can do it your way if you want," Gavin had replied, in response to my suggestion of the timesaving brainwaves of old. "You're the boss, but you'll ruin it of course."

The 'professor of bodies' was always saying, "you're the boss." Yet, if ever he disliked what we suggested, he never gave in; and invariably, regardless of the logic behind his or our reasoning, we had to succumb to Gavin's *apparent* wisdom. So the sides of the body, and therefore the edges of the doors too, would have to curve in all directions. The same applied to the tubular steel, which would have to be out of line in all directions.

At first, we thought this might make some of the work easier, as nothing would have to be exact. Not a bit of it: if the shaping of a steel member at the rear was out of line in one direction by much more than Des's two millimetres, the natural curve created could head off and dissect the bottom of the spare wheel. Alternatively, an error the other way could create a line that met up with its opposite number somewhere beyond the back bumper. Understandably, neither was particularly desirable for an intended stylish body.

We also soon discovered that we were unable to use thin-walled, easy-to-bend tube. However carefully we tried, the tube just kinked. Forming the tighter curves using a hydraulic commercial pipe-bender was easy enough with thicker tube but the gentle flowing curves were quite another matter. The three of us, Bill, Jack and I, had had to position the required piece of tube across two wooden blocks placed a few inches apart; then, while one of us moved the tube back and forth lengthways, another beat it hard between the two blocks and the third, usually me, had to keep an eye on the effective smoothness of the curve. Eventually, the desired shape – due mainly to Bill's persever-ance, Jacks precision and the Roadster's apparent natural luck – would fit the template we were attempting to match.

All this was a constant reminder of when my friend and I, as children, had flattened that piece of corrugated iron with a club hammer. That too had been in order to create an apparent exotic body, albeit for a box-cart. Now, all these years later, I was sure there must be a better way, especially with modern machinery; but, in our ignorance, we battled on.

At least the little trunk lid would be easy enough. We would just make up its framework, complete with lock and hinges, 'as one' with the rear framework and then cut out the finished, fully-operational lid. "Very clever," said Jack when Bill explained this one evening. Was it just? More like another of those mini-nightmares. By the time we had finished our *clever* idea, the little trunk lid, with all its extremities, jammed in all manner of positions; and when we checked how the lid would open with the spare wheel and tyre in place, it simply would not.

I could well visualise the scene: "Hang on while we remove the spare wheel so we can open the trunk." Better still, with the Seville's fancy electric release: "Hang on while I remove the spare wheel, so I can push the amazing button in the glove compartment to open the trunk." At times like this, we felt some dark cloud had descended to engulf us, leaving us battered and broken, mentally spewed across the rough concrete floor of a remote and unfriendly barn.

Mulling over this particular, apparently insurmountable problem, I remembered our company's patented low-friction hinges. Having for the life of us wondered where, as requested by the other shareholders, they could successfully be applied, just possibly this was it. Operating on tubular supports, their rolling action would tend to lift the rear of the lid, which was exactly what was needed. To our pleasant surprise, not only did they lift the lid clear of the spare, but the hinge's near-fric-tionless nature was a bonus too. There was no stiffness, which meant our little lid was much easier to open from the side, its only point of access. That was one of those rare 'silver lining' days: two problems solved in one.

Then, one evening, while fitting the last of the tubular framework to the rear, the Roadster's true shape suddenly appeared. The change was quite startling. We all three stood there, in silent awe. We stopped,

81

retired to the deck chairs and just sat and gazed. I think we knew, as we continued admiring our handiwork, that we had turned a major corner. It gave us a huge boost and, from that day on, no matter what hours we worked, Saturdays often becoming the early hours of Sundays, we never seemed to tire: it even gave a boost to our normal everyday work too.

The boost was certainly needed when we got back to those dratted doors. As always, left until last, we discovered that whatever needed to be done to the edges of the doors had also to be done to the surrounding sides of the body: in front, behind and below. The whole lot had to line up exactly so that the aluminium panelling would flow from the bulkhead across the doors and onto the rear without any mismatch. The Professor's insistence that everything be curved in all directions was a nightmare, for ever compounded by his chitty-chatty nature on the telephone as if everything was a bit of a joke. If nothing else, he certainly had faith in us: either that or he was as mad as we were probably insane.

As we neared the end, one afternoon, I received a concerned call from Bill.

"I've just been down to the barn, and its been broken into," he exclaimed.

"What!" I interjected, "What's happened, is anything missing?" Then, fearing this was possibly the work of vandals, I quickly added: "Is there any damage?

"I don't know. I haven't been inside. The hasp and staple have been forced and the door is slightly ajar. I didn't want to touch anything... in case of fingerprints."

My heart sank: after all these months, would this be the setback of all setbacks? However much I tried to think otherwise, the worst kept coming to the fore. There were visions of missing hard-to-find and other special pieces; I could imagine a vandalised stainless-steel radiator cowl and headlamp bar, to say nothing of missing headlamps and other expensive items. At the very least, I could visualise the contents of those sealed plastic bags littering the concrete floor, thrown aside in someone's desperate search for something of value.

"You telephone the police and I'll contact Jack to see if he can meet us there." I said, deciding this needed group assessment.

Jack was out with a customer but I managed to find Sandy. After his initial "Oh, I'm sure it'll be alright," he agreed to meet us. I got back to Bill. He had been in touch with the police and persuaded them of the seriousness of the situation. They were sending someone to the barn right away.

Twenty minutes later, three, silent, would-be auto-engineers stood outside the barn, the conversation never advancing beyond the irrelevant. None of us wished to vent a view, a suspicion or a theory on what we would find inside. Whatever we did discover was bound to be unwelcome.

The tall detective-inspector arrived and checked the door for prints. "What," he politely enquired, "was of such special value inside this none-too-special barn." The more we explained the splendour and rarity of what lay inside, the more sceptical and confused he became. The fingerprinting done, Bill pulled the door to one side.

We walked in. A loud click was heard as Bill pushed the old metal toggle light-switch and the dull glow of the vaguely improved lighting spread across the barn floor and partway up those darkly painted corrugated iron walls.

There was silence; in time broken only by the detective-inspector, with mounting confusion, enquiring of me, still in a suit having come straight from the office:

"Well, what's missing... what's happened?"

I stared in disbelief, as did the heavy-jerseyed Bill. At which, Sandy, in short-sleeved shirt and tie as always, who had not been down to the barn for some time, launched forth with his usual forthright zeal.

"Gosh! Isn't it fantastic... what a machine, wow!" he exclaimed, as he advanced towards the structure.

I saw the look of bafflement on the officer's face turn to mild irritation at both sight and sound of this odd trio. Just in time, I checked Sandy from uttering another of his prolonged eulogies over our barely recognisable motorcar.

"Yes?" said the officer, looking partly at Sandy and partly at me, and throwing an odd glance at Bill, "but what's missing... what's happened?"

Bill, if to be judged by the vacant look he now exuded, had no intention of replying. I, apparently, would have to inform the troubled officer of the true situation.

"The fact is," I said, dividing my attention equally between the floor and the now somewhat terse detective-inspector, "it looks the same as we left it. I can't see anything missing or that anything has been disturbed."

The friendly officer could only scratch his head and sport a bemused smile. Then, while we kept Sandy's eyes diverted from his unfinished toy, we thanked the kind lawman for his time and he went on his way.

Apart from an old electric drill and a new battery, both of which had been left near the door, not a thing had been touched. All the expensive electric tools, intermingled with the apparent useless motoring junk, had, very luckily, been out of sight.

In truth, it would have taken quite some imagination for any self-respecting burglar to believe there was anything of value in the barn: other than, just possibly, some large shiny objects firmly attached to a blackened structure sitting solidly in the middle of the rough concrete floor. These, much to our relief, would appear to have been no more removable than they were off-loadable.

We had to laugh at our stupidity: that we could have thought anyone, other than ourselves, would perceive the slightest value in our half-finished creation. Still, it could have been disastrous and we were appreciative of our good fortune. With that, we headed for the nearest pub to relax.

Despite this interruption, and despite the delays caused by mini-trunks and maxi-doors and all the other lesser nuisances, we eventually completed every bit that Gavin had requested. That included the tubular framework itself, the structure at the base of the up-and-over bonnet, the new rear wing fixing-bars above the rear mudguards and the additions to the roof needed to meet up with the rear and the top of the door windows.

Challenging and educational as the exercise had been, it was – as Bill put it – "no doddle." Nor, I might say, was it the sort of task, normally, for which I would have raised my hand and volunteered; and Jack, precise and accurate as he could only always be, found the whole thing thoroughly crude and messy.

When the time came for the car to be taken to Gavin, this time there was no ceremony: we were taking no chances. The now fully-structured blackened hulk was just trundled away, sitting, as before, high on Bill's trailer. I followed close behind, in the ever-faithful Jaws, sincerely hoping, as did we all, that young Gavin would not tell us we had done it all wrong; or, worse still, that he had acquired eleventh-hour jitters and cop out after all.

8. What Now Boss?

"Well, what do you think?" I asked when we arrived.

"It's all right," Gavin said, as he cast an eye in the direction of Bill's trailer. Then, with a wry smile: "I said you could do it and you have."

After introducing Bill, who eyed the young body-builder with mild suspicion through his horn-rimmed glasses, we headed off to inspect the newly made wing bucks. Gavin's workspace, in strict contrast to Des's, had barely enough room to squeeze in the smallest of classic cars, let alone an occasional Rolls-Royce or the odd Roadster. Its only redeeming feature, at one end and to one side, was an alcove housing a forming wheel and a guillotine, two all-important tools of the body-builder's trade, which just left enough space for some actual panel forming.

As I walked in, I noticed the previously neat and tidy workshop was not so very neat and tidy any more. In fact, bits of bodywork, hand tools and pieces of semi-formed sheet-metal, to say nothing of hundreds of little spiralled aluminium off-cuts, littered the floor for as far as the eye could see. I presumed the change of ambience was due to pressure of work and made no comment.

Having viewed the wing bucks, we off-loaded our structured hulk into a large shed nearby. Inside, a range of haphazardly parked semi-dismantled exotica reminded me rather too much of those other coachbuilders where Gavin and I had first met. I closed my mind to any possible negatives and, with formalities over, Bill and I made our separate ways home.

There was still no respite from the ongoing work. On the one hand, Bill had to adapt the housing for the ventilating fan to fit under the new narrower but taller bonnet. His alterations to this awkwardly-shaped fibreglass moulding would not only have to cater for the correct airflow but, being visible with a side-opening bonnet, would also have to aspire to reasonable artistry.

My priority was to organise the electrical alterations with Alan and his ever-patient associate, and to finding someone capable of cutting and narrowing the dashboard to match the narrowed bulkhead – and without the result *looking* modified. While I had undying faith in our highly qualified electricians, I was far from sure how to achieve the desired result on the decorative dashboard, complete with all its switches, gauges, air vents and telltale warning lights. Nobody so far had offered any ideas or even indicated whether they thought it possible.

First, I studied the mass of wiring sitting on the sheet of chipboard in the barn, then I looked at the clean, professional lines of the dashboard, still wrapped neatly in its clear plastic bag. I decided to start on the dashboard: the wires could wait.

I took the complex moulded bit of interior to see what our precision engineer thought. Jack's assessment was that such a delicate job would somehow have to be tackled using a scalpel on the plastic outside and a hacksaw on its metal centre. He agreed that the finished product would be of little use if there were even the slightest hint of its having been attacked with a blunt kitchen knife. There were, however, no volunteers amongst Jack or his staff to carry out the operation.

A little despondent, I went home and marked the cut-lines with a pencil on the back, on the front and on the underneath; and sat contemplating. Having looked blankly at the fine pencil lines every evening after work for several days, cowardice won. I put the piece of curvaceous plastic to one side and returned to the spider's web. The dashboard could wait.

I went off to see Alan with a set of the Seville's original wiring diagrams and the list of modifications needed to cater for the rear doors being used as forward-opening fronts, for only two doors instead of four and for the new positions of the exterior lights.

"Well," said Alan, tugging at an ill-fitting sleeve of another of his brightly coloured anoraks, "why not lend us a hand? You know the Seville so well... it would make the job much easier and quicker."

"I don't mean," he continued, seeing my look of concern, "that we are concerned about doing the work... certainly not. All that's needed is to supply a reliable source of power to all the original components but in their new positions." He paused, then continued: "If you can spend time checking the components against the diagrams, while we get on with the alterations, that in itself would be a great help."

Here, again, was some of the ball being thrown back into my court. Yet, to give Alan his due, he was making everything appear so simple, so obvious. Nevertheless, by the sound of what he was saying and the way he was saying it, he had still not entirely forgotten that regretted *mundane* remark.

"All right, if you think that will be of help." Then, before letting them completely off the hook, added: "But if I'm going to join in and advise... and it can only be late afternoons and evenings... you must at least give me something useful to do as well? I can't just sit around while you do all the work."

"Certainly," Alan said, with apparent delight at his persuasive success, then chipping in with: "You could always help with some of the soldering... you could easily do that if we showed you how."

We got together a couple of days later to mark up the changes, then on odd afternoons and evenings, I took on my latest role: that of Electrical Assistant to the Electrical Engineers. At least, with three of us, we should finish everything well before the car returned from Gavin's.

When next I visited Gavin, he had begun on the rear wings and was about to start on the panelling around the trunk. No sooner had I put my head around the door, than the young professor of bodies launched into a scolding attack:

"There's a problem with your plans," he said, pointing to the large set now pinned on the wall to one side of the guillotine. "Look at this here. You've got the front end far too high and the back end isn't correct either... and you've drawn this template for the front wing buck all wrong too."

I looked at the plans, I looked at the car and I looked back at Gavin.

"What seems to be the problem?" I said.

"Well, look here," he replied, picking up a tape measure and advancing on the car.

He put the end of the tape on the ground and measured up to the top of the forward end of the right hand space-frame: "If you check this point compared to the drawings, it's miles out."

I had never given it much thought. Gavin was obviously so used to unmoving rigid old-time suspensions that he had no idea what happened when six hundred pounds of engine and transmission, to say nothing of the components and all the other metal-work, were removed from the front of a modern soft-sprung car, especially an American one.

"Good grief," I said, "the springs are *way up*, especially at the front. That measurement bears no relation to where the car will eventually sit relative to the ground. Take the wheels off and I'll show you."

Jack, Bill and I knew only too well the effect of removing the wheels and supporting the car on stands at its correct ride height. We had always done this as a double check when making up the framework. Also, when positioned thus, and with a bit of imagination, it was possible visually to 'clothe' the framework for the 'sleek machine' to appear. Afterwards, in your mind's eye, the 'sleek machine' tended to stay, whether at the correct ride height or not. Young Gavin and his even younger assistant, Graham, must have convinced themselves that our plans were an optical conjuring trick and that the result would never resemble the graceful flowing lines as depicted on the wall.

"I know what you mean," said Gavin, "I can visualise it. We don't need to take the wheels off... anyway, we need them on to move it."

"Come on," I said, "I'll help you put them on again afterwards."

Reluctantly, Gavin agreed and, having located four axle-stands, the 'two Gs' removed the wheels and lowered the structure to the correct height above the floor. Finished, they walked away and turned.

"Wow!" exclaimed Gavin, "I would never have believed it. That really is going to be some car!"

Graham remained silent: either he was less impressed or more reserved. Anyway, the two of them soon discovered, just as we had, that without the wheels there was a constant ready reference, both visually and factually; so, for the most time while there, the wheels remained firmly *off*.

The other problem, the one with the front wing buck, was entirely the fault of the drawer of plans – and never was I allowed to forget it. I had completely miss-drawn one of the wing cross-sections and the result was an embarrassing lump where no lump should have been.

"Sorry," I said, when the origin of the error had been tracked down. "I told you not to have too much faith in us," adding, mostly in jest I hoped, "You are bound to discover any number of our mistakes as you get going!"

Then, looking more closely at the buck, I remembered another concern that Bruce and Frank had long since had. The design of the front wings, where in one sweep they sloped forwards, inwards and downwards towards the bumpers, appeared not to work.

"We've always wondered about this area," I said. "and none of us have been able to find a picture of a car with such front wings. Maybe it's just not possible."

"Any shape is possible in aluminium," Gavin replied, with one of his all-knowing looks. "You'll see... wait till we get to that part."

Then I noticed, yet again, the state of the workshop, as well as the state of the yard outside. The whole place was even more disorganised and untidy than when we delivered the car. This time I felt inclined to comment.

The truth eventually emerged. Gavin had only ever tidied up once: that was in order to demonstrate his apparent super-efficiency over and above his undoubted expertise. On that same occasion, Graham had arrived for work without having shaved, at which Gavin had immediately sent him home to do so. Graham, it transpired, had never been sure who to blame: Gavin or me. In time, thankfully, he came to blame Gavin.

With the ongoing verbal struggle between the young and the not-so-young, I made the best of the revelation. I somehow needed to keep my end up. Still, as time progressed, the unlikely alliance developed into a well-balanced two-sided banter; and a good bit of teamwork too.

A reasonable all-round, self-taught engineer I might have been, but a bodybuilder in multi-shaped aluminium, I most certainly was not.

These meetings, about once every ten days, always had their interests. On my arrival, Gavin and I would run through the plans, discussing the bits that he had done and thrashing out details on those about to be done. I always looked forward to seeing the progress, as well as knowing that something challenging would crop up.

Having decided to start at the tail end, Gavin was working forward from there. Why, I have no idea, but it seemed as good a way as any. The doors would be the exception: these would only be 'skinned' after Gavin had completed the decorative swage lines fore and aft as a guide for those on the door.

I soon realised I was witnessing art in the making: complex creations in shaped sheet metal, and taking place, literally, as I watched. A bit of aluminium was roughly cut out, put through the body-builder's wheel to be rolled until the desired flowing curve appeared, then, if the piece was a part of the body, it was placed in position on the tubular framework or, if part of a wing, onto the relevant buck. After which, the edges were either cut to match to the previous piece, or left ready to mate with the following one. Finally, the whole lot was welded together as though stitching up a bit of clothing. The simplicity was a deception – it also had its moments.

"How are you going to attach the back wings, boss?"

"Boss!" There it was again. The so-called boss was mostly told to go and check and modify his plans, produce some other measurement or re-draw a suspect template. The more I heard the elevated title, the more I knew I was not.

"What do you mean? What have I or we done wrong now?" I asked.

"Well, look at this," he said, pointing to the Seville's rear mudguard, "how do you expect me to fit the rear end around here, or the back wings on either for that matter?"

I looked, and realised that no account had been taken of how the rear panelling was to be folded around the edge of the shaped bar under which the wings were to be fitted. In effect, there was so little space between the top of the old mudguards and the underside of the bar that barely a finger could be squeezed in, let alone a hammer to fold the aluminium.

"You'll have to remove the mudguards," Gavin insisted.

"You've got another think coming," I instinctively replied.

As Lionel had confirmed on one of his visits, the rear mudguards were an integral structural part of the overall construction and therefore could not be removed. Then, realising what was brewing, I quickly stormed in: "Gavin, as unusual as these inner steel mudguards might be on this style of car, not only will they stop the mud and stones destroying your pretty wings from underneath, but they also happen to be part of the strength of the structure. Regardless of all or any of your persuasive arguments, they have to stay... and that's final."

"Well, we can't possibly fit the back end on as it is," he retorted with a hint of irritation.

"That's a pity," I replied, "you'll just have to forgo the elegant tail we've taken so much time designing, and put some sort of 'pickup' rear-end on instead."

That had a ring of nostalgia. I would always be reminded of that first sighting of the Chicken Manure Special: one of those car-cum-pickups heading off into the distance with its trunk open and laden with muck. Gavin had to laugh and, in this one instance at least, he knew, under no circumstances, could we succumb to his request.

We drew a blank at first as to what to do. In time, as with so many of these hurdles, we came up with a practical, if somewhat convoluted, idea. We drilled a number of large holes through the mudguards in line with the steel bar above and, through these, Gavin used a metal drift to fold over the edge of the body panelling. Afterwards, having lined up suitable threaded holes with the large holes, we bolted on the wings using a socket spanner. To keep the dirt out, the holes would eventually be plugged with large push-in plastic bungs as supplied by the electricians.

The idea had its moments but worked well enough and, in the end, Gavin forgave us for our lack of foresight and me, as he unkindly put it, for my pedantic goings-on.

Later, when it came to making the forward end of the front wings, Gavin hit a problem just as we had suspected. This area – not much more than a foot square – ended up giving Gavin his greatest challenge; and, every time he complained, I merely repeated back to him his own words of: "'any shape is possible in aluminium', you said."

"Yes boss," he would reply, in a drawn out dry sort of way, finishing off with, "I heard you the first time!"

Despite this, he eventually produced what was needed. Yet, as always, he would soon get his own back.

"Give us a hand boss," he would often call out, on occasions holding the acetylene torch in one hand and piece of panelling in the other. I would grab hold at some point with meaningful determination, at which, aluminium being such a good heat conductor, I would let out a violent expletive. At this, instead of showing a modicum of understanding or sympathy, he would merely say: "Just because it's not glowing, doesn't mean it's not hot!"

More than once, I was caught and, each time, the statement was repeated with increasing glee: and always accompanied by that cheeky grin, peering, irreverently, from behind the protective goggles. It quickly became a latter-day reminder of those burned fingers when attempting to heat-treat that questionable wired-up timing chain on the University Buick.

Still, despite this, and the many other hazards likely to befall a novice in his later years, I survived my time with the two Gs. In fact, with the ongoing un-catered for complications, the days became ever more drawn. There were times when a fish and chip dinner at nine o'clock ended with our parting at two in the morning. There were times also when Gavin's landlord arrived with late-night refreshments, as often as not showing due concern for our health: extreme mental, in my case, I suspect. Nevertheless, little by little, a piece at a time, the smooth and curvaceous art-form steadily engulfed our blackened, angular hulk.

We were making good progress back home too. Bill had finished the fan housing, along with a number of other fiddly but essential jobs, and Alan and I were plotting a steady course with the wiring. The engine loom alterations were now complete, as well as the greatly modified ones for the doors. We were now working on the looms that ran from under the dashboard to the rear, all of which simply needed shortening.

Alan, while fiddling with the sleeve of his ill-fitting anorak, handed me one to shorten and re-solder – I had now progressed to cutting and joining as well. Having done this in Alan's prescribed 'staggered' format – the joins being at varying positions along the loom – I started soldering. The wires were unusual, I thought. They were not the normal multi-strand ones but single strand and rather soft. Still, not for me to wonder why and I set to with the soldering.

I was getting quite good at this now. First, place the join on top of a small wooden block so that nothing untoward was burned and the heat only went into the wires. Next, put the tip of the iron firmly on the join and pull the trigger-switch. Then, when hot enough, push the solder between the tip of the iron and the join. This time, however, instead of fusing onto the wires, the solder ran away onto the table, just like a host of mini ball-bearings.

I had obviously not heated the wires long enough. Try again and hold the iron on for longer. There was still no luck, just the same. I had another go: no change, just lots of little silver bubbles. What a waste of solder, I thought: the bubbles were everywhere now, even over-flowing onto the floor.

"What's the problem?" Alan asked, on hearing the strained mumbling at my end of the workbench.

"It's these damned wires," I said. "They won't join together. The solder won't stick to them. It's most odd!"

He came across, took hold of the loom, felt the wires, scratched away at their surface, and then bent them individually back and forth. He looked up, grinning.

"Of course you can't solder them," he said, "they're aluminium. How odd, I wonder why they used aluminium in this one loom?"

"Well?" I enquired with some irritation, quite disinterested as to why aluminium had been used: "What now boss?" Two, I decided, could play at Gavin's game.

"Don't worry," he replied, seeing my obvious frustration, "we've a couple of options. Either we use aluminium solder, which is difficult to work with, or we change the wires in the loom to multi-strand copper."

We did the latter. It took ages; undoing all the little end-connectors from the junctions in the loom and soldering them back onto new, correct colour-coded multi-strand copper wires. Whatever possessed someone to use aluminium in this one loom, in amongst all those miles of wires, we will no doubt never know. When finished, we had clocked up another string of hours to an apparently ever-growing schedule.

With the wiring complete, it was time to return to the dashboard. Having drawn those fine pencil lines on that pristine bit of interior long before starting on the wiring, I was still nervous of wielding a scalpel or hacksaw to this irreplaceable piece of upper dashboard. Any mistake, and Des, for sure, would blame me for ruining *his* car.

The more I looked at the long curved metal-reinforced plastic complexity, the more I realised this was no easy undertaking, and certainly not for a novice. Not only did several inches have to be removed from the middle and the two halves rejoined, but the same also had to be done to all the other pieces, both seen and unseen. There were the idiot warning lights, mini air-conditioning ducts, hazard warning buzzers and even the 'ding-dong' seat-belt chimes to be considered. The intricacies of this not-too-large bit of automobile seemed never ending. So, it was a case of "no spectators please" and of that I made sure. Armed with the correct implements, I set myself up in the garage, locked the door and started dissecting.

Of all the bits on that irreplaceable upper dashboard, the worst has to have been the two chrome vertically-grilled air vents that had to be made into an elongated single piece. Each had to have their opposite ends removed and then invisibly joined as one. As always, nothing was straight, so each had to be cut at a slight angle, which more than trebled the time. Then, to finish off the little complexity, I had to use a magnifying glass to shape and fit the tiny centre grille bar. Was this, I thought as I laboured away, dedication to a cause, an illness – contagious or otherwise – or just plain insanity?

The ordeal over, Bill and I set to on the one last chore before the Roadster's, hoped for, triumphant return. Having decided since the break-in at the barn to complete the project in our own not-too-large double garage, all the stored components needed to be moved from barn to garage. While doing so, each had to be checked and cleaned and any necessary replacement parts ordered from Bob in Ohio. When complete, we re-sealed them in their individual clear plastic bags and hung them on the overhead beams in the garage. There they accumulated, one by one, looking like some obscure 'name the part' game awaiting the car's return.

Gavin and Graham's job was now almost done too. They only had to finish edging the trunk and door openings, make the front apron that joined the front wings together between the bumper and the grille and complete the up-and-over bonnet.

As I arrived on my last but one visit, I noticed the four pieces of the bonnet sitting to one side of the body shop – all very exciting. Yet something struck me as odd about the sides. Still, old-time bonnets standing on end like some misaligned fire screen would look odd at the best of times. There was work to do: the bonnet could wait.

Then, as Gavin was about to check and copy detail for the weatherproofing from Jaws' trunk, I began to suspect what was odd about the sides of the bonnet. I wandered over to take a closer look. I saw Graham eye me as I did so: he knew something too. Yes, that was the narrower front and, yes, that was the outside with the pressed-out decorative swage line along the top – and, yes, that was the problem. Graham obviously knew too but had no intention of being the first to bear the news.

"Gavin," I said. "What are you trying to do... air-condition the engine compartment or something?"

"What do you mean boss?" He answered with a grin as he walked over to see what I was about.

"The louvres," I said, "look how they're angled." Then, half-jokingly: "you'll not only air-condition the engine compartment, you'll pressurise the underside of bonnet so that it'll blow clean off... we'll leave it in the middle of a motorway on our first run!"

Whoever Gavin had contracted to press out the louvres had done them the wrong way round: instead of the air around the engine flowing out through the louvres, outside air would be forced in.

The sense of humour failure that followed was of the silent muttering type, followed by, once outside, a string of expletives. The young professor of bodies did not much care for learning by his mistakes, or anyone else's for that matter, any more than I had with the University Buick and others. Yet, I felt for him. Where I had learnt on some fairly worthless elderly transport, he would now end up having to make *four* bonnet sides for a *two*-sided car.

As a lasting memento of his frustration, there are a number of character marks on the replacements, and, as keepsakes, I have one of those super-cooling works of art and Gavin kept the other.

In the end, with Graham's help, Gavin finished clothing our all-black multi-structured hulk on Christmas Eve. This meant that he had not only managed to complete the work in the time promised, but he had also done it for the same price as first quoted by those other best-forgotten coachbuilders. In fairness though, having seen the complexities involved, we had to have a modicum of sympathy for that previous team's capitulation. One thing for sure, though: those two young lads – who had succeeded where others had failed – deserved medals for perseverance alone.

It was one o'clock on Christmas Eve morning when Gavin, sporting one of his cheekiest of smiles, and Bill, having arrived earlier with his trailer, began loading up the newly bodied creation. As they did so, I stood for a moment to admire the sweeping lines of Gavin's art-form. At which, with a misconceived mounting air of confidence and with blissful simplicity, kidded myself that the shiny metal monster only needed its innards put back, a coat of paint and a bit of chrome; and, no sooner done, we would be off to show our creation to the world – more wishful thinking in the extreme.

9. An End In Sight

I stood chatting to Tom, our mechanical expert, while eyeing the bright blue engine sitting on the floor beside us. With its gleaming black bracketry and polished aluminium transmission, this, the very heart of the Roadster, was patiently waiting to be returned to where it belonged.

Tom had rescued the once-filthy engine and transmission several months earlier from Frank's barn. Back in his smart Rover workshop, he had carried out a thorough dismantle-check-and-clean and replaced all suspect parts. Then, having masked up any openings that might not care for a mouthful of paint, he had manhandled the cast iron lump on a mobile hoist into the body-shop for a re-spray. Having sandblasted and painted the bracketry and cleaned the transmission and the alternator with wire wool and metal polish, he had put whole lot back together again.

"The job had to be done right you know. It's a magnificent engine... it deserved it!" he concluded.

This was getting out of hand. What with the argumentative Des being ultra-possessive about *his* car and Gavin, with all his smiling impudence, constantly referring to *his* panelling, was the excitable Tom now to become over-attached to *his* engine? The thought was too much, and I put such possibilities firmly to one side.

We were both waiting patiently for Bill. If he failed to show up soon, there would be insufficient time to fit the engine and transmission into the Roadster before the workshop shut at midday for the Christmas break. Without the engine and transmission in place, we would be unable to make a start on the final re-assembly during the Christmas to New Year holidays.

Even accounting for Bill and Gavin having had a late night yarn and Bill having a couple of extra roll-ups, Bill should have been no more than half-an-hour behind me. Perhaps he had arrived home exhausted, gone straight to bed and overslept. I was not feeling that wide-awake myself.

"There's an aluminium *thing* on a trailer outside," someone suddenly shouted from across the workshop. "Is that what you're waiting for?"

"Is somebody referring to our exotic car as a *thing*?" I enquired with some irritation. There was no reply. Seeing for the first time in full daylight, our unpainted, part-finished creation perched tiptoes on its un-weighted suspension with chalk-marked un-cutout rear window and unchromed truck spring bumpers, I did have some sympathy for the observation. The only consolation was that Bill and the Roadster had arrived, and in one piece.

"What happened to you?" I asked.

"I had a slight problem," he started. "I had to stop on the motorway."

With time being short, I refrained from pressing him further and set to helping manoeuvre the car into the workshop. When, with some difficulty, we had finished fitting an oversize engine and transmission into an undersize engine compartment, we wished everybody a Happy Christmas and went on our way. Once home, the now fully clothed and fully engined machine was put to bed in our garage alongside old Jaws, ready for the re-assembly. Only then did I have a chance to find out what had happened to Bill the night before.

"Well," he said, with the merest hint of concern, "I was late because I didn't get much sleep. When I got to bed, I kept having this recurring nightmare about being overtaken by the Roadster."

He paused, then went on: "It wasn't some vision of the future... I was re-living what actually happened... I think I was in shock or something."

Eyes widening, I stayed silent as he continued: "Well, when I hit that bit of ice on the motorway... you must have come across it too... the trailer began to jack-knife. At first, it swung into the car, then... I don't know how, but the whole lot spun around and finished broadside across all three lanes." He paused, then, "So you see... 'the Roadster overtook me'." Again he paused, and I, unable to gather any rational thoughts, remained speechless. So he continued: "I still don't remember how I managed to get out of the way before the next car came along."

By this time, I was beyond speechless: I was semi-mesmerised. Disaster! Wipeout! If not for having been in the early hours of the morning when that notorious longest ring-road in the world has a minimum of traffic – and there being hardly any trucks out on

Christmas Eve – a Roadster-to-be might never have been, to say nothing of Bill, his car and his trailer. Whether or not somebody's watchful eye from on high had played a part, who knows? In the end, I guess I suffered as much from shock as Bill; and we both retired inside to a comforting pre-Christmas drink.

Our all brick garage, although wider than average, was a tight fit even for one large car, let alone two; and the area where we would have to work, even with Jaws moved out into the drive, was not much more than at Gavin's. Therefore, anything not needed had been put in the loft up the stairs at the back, leaving only the serried rows of re-bagged components hanging from the ceiling joists and some builder's props, a few lengths of wood and a bicycle relegated to one corner.

That evening, while carefully studying our newly completed dull-aluminium creation and as the initial excitement of the Roadster's long-awaited triumphant return subsided, I realised that Gavin's panelling was not quite to the standard that might reasonably have been expected. Parts of the front wings looked as though the Three Bears had been playing pat-a-cake on them and various bits seemed not to line up as they should, to say nothing of the crude seventies hinges protruding through some roughly-cut holes in the lower rear corners of the doors.

As the implications slowly sank in, so did the euphoria slowly dissipate; and one of those dark clouds started to settle. Gavin, presumably, had done his best and that was that, or had he?

To be fair, the unsightly door hinges were mostly of our doing. The tremendous strength of the Seville's door hinges, with their 'stops' and 'hold-opens', to say nothing of their ability to be bolted straight back on, had persuaded me – and eventually Bill and Jack too – that they should be retained. We had merely assumed that Gavin would find some neat way to cover them.

Visions of failed Ferrari-cum-Corvettes raised their head again: the pinprick from university days returning to the fore. Not a word, though, did I divulge over Christmas; but, immediately after, I collared Gavin on the telephone.

"Don't worry boss," came echoing, unconcerned down the line. "It just needs a bit of finishing off. I'll come up at the weekend and sort it all out. Have no fears, boss."

"Don't worry" – "have no fears" – "I'll sort it all out over a weekend." I had heard that all too often before. For all I knew, over one weekend, Gavin could make things even worse. A state of mild panic set in. I would never live this down; and no one was going to smile blandly and sanction more money to cure what a twenty-year-old had been let loose on.

I began to think the unthinkable: that it might have been better – provided Bill and his car had somehow been left unscathed – if a lorry had run over our budding masterpiece in the early hours of Christmas Eve after all. That would have put an end to these fraught Christmas to New Year holiday breaks: last year a bit of misaligned steering, this year a whole misaligned body.

Gavin came and did his "weekend" and, as suspected, barely made a start. The wings of his art-form required the most inordinate amount of bashing with a piece of old cut-off flat spring he called a 'flapper'. Aimed with a gentle stroking motion, this *essential* tool of the trade was used to finish off any rounded aluminium work. If so, why had I not seen it before?

Bill and I, meantime, while trying to ignore the body problems, plodded on during weekday evenings with the re-assembly. Then, early each Friday, Gavin, cheerful as always, would arrive, stay on Friday night, and work through until Saturday evening. This continued, week after week, well into February. Slowly, bit-by-bit, the bodywork improved and we began to feel some confidence creeping back.

When it came to the door hinges, we all set to and designed a mating two-piece cover, one half for the door and the other half for the panel behind. With the first pair in place, Gavin stood back, admired his handiwork and proclaimed with one of his more stupid grins: "Yes boss, very sexy, very sexy indeed!"

To which, in the best traditions of Captain Mainwaring of 'Dad's Army', I simply gave him a withering look and said: "Stupid Boy!" At which, for some inexplicable reason, I received no reply; and, with the grin unaltered, the *boy* got on with the task in hand.

On his final weekend, the young professor, in order to make a final check of the wheel openings in the wings – and no doubt in order to liven things up – requested the car be set at its correct ride height, but without removing the wheels.

"How can we do that?" Bill asked, with a nonchalant rub of the chin. "The car is still several hundred pounds light... and the front springs haven't been altered yet to compensate for its eventual overall reduced weight."

"It's got to be done," said Gavin, "it's the only way to be sure the wheel-arch openings are correct."

To remove any springs was out of the question. We had long since discovered just how long this took. "As bad as dealing with that spider's web of a wiring harness," Alan, had complained when helping remove the front coils prior to the sandblasting, ever-fearful that one of them would de-compress and fly across the barn, leaving a trail of destruction in its wake.

"There's a load of bricks out the back," I said to nobody in particular, then added, "But surely we don't have to fill the car with bricks... that would be ridiculous."

As I rambled on, mostly to myself, I spied the three wind-up builders' props resting in the corner, leftover from some do-it-yourself building work.

"Would it be possible," I suggested, thinking as I spoke, "to force the car down on its suspension by putting the builder's props between the car and the joists up above?"

A stony silence was accompanied by withering looks to match, interrupted only by the barely perceptible buzz of the fluorescent lights overhead. Bill was the first to speak: "Why not? The bumpers are designed for jacking the car *up*, so they should be capable of jacking it *down*."

Duly encouraged, I chipped in with: "Hopefully, there's enough junk in the loft above not to jack the roof off instead!"

After further withering looks, two of the props were placed on the front bumper and the third, which we hoped would prove man enough on its own, was positioned at the rear. All three were adjusted to reach the appropriate beams overhead; and wound up – or *down*, as the case may be. Using a tape measure to note the reducing distance between bumper and floor, down the car went; and one of the Young Professor's more awkward requests was fulfilled by one of the Boss's better brainwaves.

We continued this final session through all of Saturday and Sunday, finishing Gavin's finishing-off in the early hours of Monday morning. Tough going, yes, but when finished, we liked what we saw. At which, with another panic over and another near-disaster averted, we sent the young professor amicably on his way.

Why we ever doubted Gavin, I have no idea. Not only did he sort out the multitude of problems, but he also refused further payment. Looking back, I think he knew that there was more work to be done. He just wanted to make out that he could keep to the original deadline – that he could do no wrong. Like everyone else, though, the young professor was human after all.

I must confess, by now, any fervour had seriously flagged. The constant workload, over and above other day-to-day responsibilities, had become almost too much. I developed a love-hate relationship with both car and project. Bill, also, with his double workload, was beginning to feel the same. The problem was that most of the work now was so tedious and time-consuming and the whole thing had gone on relentlessly, evenings and weekends, for nearly two years.

Often, if one of our ideas solved some obscure problem with the re-fitting, there was every likelihood that the same brainwave would hinder something else, or even cause another unrelated and quite unexpected problem; while continually remembering too that everything had to be properly repairable and maintainable. Many a time we were tempted just to weld or rivet an item in place; it would have been so much easier. Indeed, such was the difficulty encountered on one occasion that a bracket, no bigger than one's thumb, took nearly as long to make and fix in place as the massive engine cross-member had on the half-chassis.

Accordingly, when unable to find what we needed in our salvaged Seville fixings, one of us would head off to 'Willy's'. Willy and his band of helpers supplied local industry with hundreds and thousands of nuts, bolts and screws, and much else besides. With our constant meagre requests, I hardly think we were his most lucrative customers, but he never once complained.

"How many do you want this time," he would ask, "one or two?"

"No, a whole four for this job," might occasionally be our reply; and sometimes even a dozen or more.

To add to our popularity, if the unusual specials we ordered were not collected as soon as they arrived, Willy's warehouseman, who looked after the place on Saturdays, would delight in selling them to someone else. Having turned the place half upside down to no avail, Willy would have to go through the ordering all over again. Still, such incidents invariably caused more amusement than inconvenience.

Then there was Paul, the recommended trimmer. We were still not sure whether he would agree to tackle the interior. Would he really be prepared to cram his stocky frame, now in its sixtieth somewhat irascible year, into that tiny cab and mess about with all those complex Seville fittings?

"Well, a car's a car, isn't it?" he said, when first setting eyes on our part-primered semi-completed machine. "They're only bits of metal, you know... be they Ferraris, Minis, Caddys or whatever." Then, shaking his head and turning to take a second look: "Well, I suppose *that's* a car too!"

I have never been quite sure whether the remark was a backhanded compliment or a straight insult. Still, at least he was talking: he could just as easily have taken a fleeting look, turned and left. He nearly had a fit when we suggested using best soft-top material on the roof. Not that he objected to such material being used merely for decoration: there was very little involved. No, the type of cloth used on soft-tops is un-stretchable, so, instead of having some leeway when covering a normally flexible framework, he would have to cut out and stitch the material to the utmost accuracy to fit the shape of a solid roof.

No sooner had he started on the interior roof lining than: "Who's the clever one who welded this great piece of iron along the inside here?" followed by, "How exactly, may I ask, am I supposed to fix the headlining all around this piddling little hole at the back that you call a window?"

He was even less amused when asked to fit out the trunk: "You want me to carpet inside that dark little hole... and with the original *black* carpeting? You never told me that. You must be joking. I can't even see into the thing, let alone measure up to cut and fit it properly!"

There was still no let up when he came to the doors: "Do you realise that the backings for the door trims, with their decorative shapes and their armrests and little courtesy lights, are stamped out on specially formed presses. You can't just re-shape this stuff... it'll take forever to alter and match up to your new shape."

Once he had let off steam, and Bill and I and any others around had smiled benignly, he settled down and improvised as best he could. As he neared the end, there was yet another outburst: "And do tell me, how I am supposed to modify this 'wood'? It's hollow at the back with part numbers on it, and would *melt* if given the chance. Have they run out of trees in Detroit, or something?"

Back in the seventies, all the decorative wooden panels that adorned the likes of the Seville, even the little screw covers on the panic handles, were a multitude of plastic pressings, and were quite unmodifiable. As the one to have overlooked this little intricacy, I was dispatched to have the necessary pieces made up by a cabinetmaker who, as always with the local help, excelled at the task.

Eventually, other than the soundproofing and carpets, which Bill had insisted we leave out until we had driven through a thunderstorm, Paul finished everything as skilfully as we had hoped. For all that, he still left mumbling to himself and shaking his head in a vaguely uncontrolled manner.

No sooner had he departed, than we were down at the local tyre and exhaust company. First, we exchanged the grubby whitewall tyres for a brand new set of the best. After which, having bolted on the newly made team-designed exhaust manifolds – modified by another 'welder of the impossible' – we had the new exhaust system fitted.

Having long since discovered at university that large American V8 engines without silencers are not particularly sociable, our newfound toy was soon being raced around the drive, driven across the lawn and even manoeuvred between flowerbeds. After nearly two years and all that hassle, why not? Why not? Because the Back-up announced that if we continued with our kindergarten behaviour the backing-up would cease forthwith. We did as told, throttled back and readied for the next stage: final assembly.

When the time came on a clear sunny day, we parked the Roadster in the middle of the drive and scattered the various body components in a seemingly orderly fashion on the adjoining lawn. Then, mindful of Des's freshly applied two-tone blue paint, Bill, as the expert, and I, the steadily improving helper, set about putting it all together. By mid-afternoon, everything except the rear wings had been fitted.

"What do you think?" I asked, with a note of excitement.

"It looks alright, doesn't it?" said Bill.

"What do you mean *alright*," I interjected. "I certainly never thought it would look quite like this."

"Well, let's wait and see what its like with the rear wings on," Bill suggested, normal caution continuing to the last.

Even the still tolerant Back-up, while plying us with refreshments, had appeared with a half-smile, repeating those same words I had used when first handed that auctioneer's postcard: "It's 'a fun looking machine'," to which she had quickly added: "I will definitely not be driving it, though... I hardly think you would want me to try 'taking off' in this one!"

Bill, who had heard the story of the elevated Aston, looked at me and I at him. We made no comment, merely raising an eyebrow knowingly at each other.

As the day progressed, I was even forgiven for insisting on having reversing lights on a body-style from an era before their invention. "You can't put those on a thirties-style car," several of the team had said. To which I had replied: "As the wiring caters for reversing lights and we intend to *use* the car, we should surely include them." In fact, Bill had to admit that the two chromium-plated fifties lamps found at an auto-jumble the previous summer added a certain something to Gavin's curvaceous tail.

"All right, let's finish it off," I agreed.

An hour later, with the rear wings attached and our Bugatti-style stainless steel wheel covers firmly fitted, we stepped back.

"Wow!" said Bill.

"Good grief," said I.

We stood there, looking at the sleek machine with a combination of deep satisfaction and certain awe. What we were looking at after two years and so many trials and complications, was almost unbelievable. It was quite unlike a restoration project: there before us was our own creation, never before seen. Certainly, we had always thought we would end up with something close to our plans but never really dared believe we would achieve it. The exhilaration was combined with a feeling of immense relief too: all those hours of work had not been in vain after all. There were of course a number of incorrectnesses that could, and would, be cured; but our eyes ignored them.

For the rest of the day, we continued to admire our handiwork over glasses of wine or whatever anybody, droppers-in included, wanted to drink – other than champagne. Champagne was for 'drivability day' when Lionel, the indomitable professional auto-engineer, had given the all clear.

Lionel arrived one morning a few days later to find the Roadster, all polished up and shining, waiting majestically for him in the drive, with me alongside. He sprang from his car, a beam from ear to ear, quite unable to contain his pleasure.

"Oh yes, oh yes," he said, and immediately out came the camera. He clicked away from this angle and that; he peered inside, looked under the bonnet and even inside the trunk. He, too, noticed the imperfections but, like us, decided to ignore them.

Then for the all-important drivability test: no sooner underway than he started a rambling semi-monotone, half I presumed intended for me and half for himself.

"Ride... smooth. Still a little bouncy at the front... that could be looked at."

"Braking... good. Steering... acceptable, but with a bit of oversteer... and what's that slight wandering we're getting as I speed up... I can't quite pinpoint that. There's a bit of work to be done there too."

"Cornering... good. Yes, the space-frame set-up and other stiffening has worked well."

As he rambled on, he glanced from one mirror to the other:

"Centre rear vision surprisingly good considering the small back window. I suppose it's because the window is so close to one's head... yes, that's it. Wing mirror on the left... just adequate being left-hand drive. Wing mirror on the right? That's quite useless. Ah, that's better... just swing your head backwards and look through the rear window to your right."

"Forward vision... well, I suppose it's really no different to the nineteen-thirties... and not dissimilar from driving a long-bonneted truck down – what do they call it in America – 'Route 66'!" to which he gave a great chuckle.

Then, flinging the steering from side to side, and obviously enjoying himself, he turned for home. He parked, switched off and sat looking down the bonnet for a good half minute, a smile firmly fixed on the normally deadpan face.

"Well," he concluded with a note of triumph, "the car's legal as far as I'm concerned... even if there are a few things needing attention, none of them are dangerous."

That then was his verdict: our *slightly* modified 1978 Seville had passed the engineer's test – only just, but *passed* it had. As we walked to his car for him to leave, Lionel turned, paused and, drawing himself to his full height, said: "I would like you and the others to know that I've found this project both enjoyable and interesting... and I am delighted to have been part of the team."

Taken more than a little by surprise, I barely managed a "Thank you." Then, bravery coming to the fore, I asked something we had all long wanted to know: "Tell me truthfully," I said, "what did you really think that first time you came down to the barn?"

He turned, looked me hard in the eye for a full few seconds. Realising that I wanted the truth, he answered, his voice a little muted, but deliberate all the same.

"When I returned to my office after that first visit, I had to conclude that either you were unable to appreciate what you had taken on, or you had simply taken leave of your senses... and I certainly never thought you would finish." After a pause, he went on: "But, on the other hand, you were obviously serious about what you were attempting, so I felt the least I could do was to help where I could." Then, on a lighter note: "You've delighted in proving me wrong... haven't you?"

I laughed, a hollow sort of laugh, as I realised the remark was about the best backhanded compliment any engineer could give. We had known all along that Lionel was no true believer but we had certainly not realised that, from the very outset, he had been quite such a disbeliever. Thinking about it, I suppose we should not have been overly surprised.

So, with Lionel's unequivocal blessing, I took the Roadster off to Tom for its final legal hurdle: the MoT test. Strict as I knew Tom's 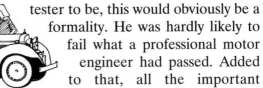 tester to be, this would obviously be a formality. He was hardly likely to fail what a professional motor engineer had passed. Added to that, all the important components on the steering, braking and suspension, along with numerous other wearing parts, had been replaced with new. I handed over the keys to Tom and sat and waited.

With the test finished, an obviously embarrassed Tom, wringing hands and swaying slowly from side to side, stood next to a grinning chief tester: "It's failed," Tom declared.

"What!" I exclaimed, staring at the chief tester. "What have you been up to now, Adolf?" I asked, using the nickname he had long since acquired due to the power he wielded over all that crossed his threshold. "The car's virtually brand new, you know!"

"It's the headlights," said Tom nervously, while Adolf continued with his grin. "The main beam is all right but there's something odd when they dip."

"Damn it," I said, "they're brand new stainless steel lamps fitted with modern halogen bulbs. The highly reputable specialist spares company we got them from would hardly supply us with *duff* headlamps, now would they?"

As I ended my dissertation, I suddenly remembered; I should have checked. Here I was getting wound up with the chief tester and I think he knew all along what I now realised. That was why he was grinning. Yes, of course it was funny: he had always said that our "concoction" should be failed the first time "just on principle".

"They dip the wrong way," I said, "don't they? The way they would in America where they drive on the other side of the road and from where the lamps were sourced. That's what's wrong, isn't it?"

His grin widened even more and his head nodded, up and down, up and down: he was ever so delighted. Tom, on the other hand, was so concerned with the failure that he took a good few seconds to realise why all the laughter. Only then did a worried frown change to a relaxed, if nervous smile.

That evening, with long-suffering Alan's help, two giant stainless-steel headlamps were dismantled and the reflectors rotated through the appropriate angle and notched. Now, just to be one up on Adolf, the headlamps can quickly and easily be changed for driving either on the left *or* the right.

The next morning the concoction was taken for a re-test. This time HLN 827V passed, returning to the road two years and three weeks after receiving that inspirational postcard, and legally registered as the same car that had been manufactured originally by GM in America. Surprisingly, as the law then stood, because of the way we had done the modifications, the only notification required by the UK licensing authority was the change of exterior colour.

That night, the champagne was opened; followed by many pints of beer in nearly as many pubs, all intermingled with much mutual patting on backs. It was during this that we discovered why farmer Frank had stayed away so long. Frank, it transpired, had never been prepared to admit – any more than I had been prepared to admit to that non-event at university – that he had once tried to alter a mass-produced, pressed-out car himself. He had concluded that such conversions were neither viable nor even possible. The first of these long-held judgements, he was not about to change, but he had to concede to the second.

"When I came to Des's," he started, "and saw how much you had cut up that car, I knew it would take you for ever – *if ever* – to get it remotely the way you wanted. I was also sure that you would eventually give up." He paused, and looked around in his normal laid back, man-of-the-land attitude to see if he was about to have issue with the silent band around him.

Having none, he continued: "Why none of you gave up, I'll never know." At which he drew a deep breath, of necessity or for effect, then went on: "As a prototype for further production, I have to admit that what you've done is quite clever. But if all those hours end up with a 'one-off', and especially if properly costed, then that's got to be the most uncommercial car I've ever seen."

Before any of us could react, he changed tack: "On the other hand, if my old father could have seen what's been produced in amongst the farm machinery in one of his grain barns, he would have been *well chuffed*." Then turning to Bill, who he had known for many years, "As for you! What ever got you involved... overgrown Morgan or not, and a *foreign* one at that... I'll never know."

Bill, not normally known for his speed of words, was instant in his reply: "Well, it's the best overgrown Morgan I've ever seen, foreign or otherwise. And it's been good fun too!"

On that note, Frank had returned to the fold. He had also given as much of a compliment as I would ever expect to pass his lips; and for that, we were all *well chuffed*. Still, as Lionel had pointed out, there was work yet to be done and, for all we knew, it might be rather more than we realised.

10. *Help!* Again

As *keeper* of the car, I was very conveniently also *driver* of the car. So, the next day, having notified the insurers and obtained a tax disc, I headed off for the nearest fast stretch of road.

My first discovery was that Bill's suggestion of leaving out the carpets and the sound proofing had been well advised. As the heavens opened and the rain bucketed down, two tiny trickles appeared on the floor: one on the driver's side and one on the passenger's. What a disaster if the soundproofing and carpets had been fitted: an un-noticed damp and mouldy mess, with its dank and musty smell, would have exuded, inexorably, from the floor. Both leaks proved easy enough to cure and, when done, Paul finished off his work; and there was no further embarrassment of the bare, unfinished metal floor.

My other discovery, as I continued the trial, was akin to a traumatic awakening. For all our theory and attention to detail, our creation did not drive or ride remotely as we had hoped. Apart from the excessive oversteer and the bounce at the front, both of which Lionel had pointed out, there were a number of other anomalies. The varying ratio steering, designed to combine precise handling at speed with near small-car manoeuvrability in urban traffic, was unnaturally twitchy up to about thirty miles an hour. Then, as the speed increased, another directional instability came into play, which came and went for no apparent reason. Finally, on rougher roads, the rear suspension bottomed out with irritating constancy.

What an unmitigated disaster. Regardless of how stylish our Roadster might be, we could hardly rush around singing its praises or offering it up as some sort of exotic prototype with qualities such as these. There was more work to be done, all right, and very likely far more than envisaged: the champagne should never have been opened.

One by one, I demonstrated the problems to the others. There were no brainwaves, no sudden inspirations. Sandy, instantly declared: "It's fantastic... just a few little problems to cure... no worries... you'll see." Yet again, glitches thrown to one side as an irrelevance: a seriously misaligned steering shaft in the early days at the barn and now, worse still, some seriously misaligned aimability.

This, all the others said, was Lionel's department: he would know what to do. When contacted, Lionel suggested we look at the steering for wear or looseness, then check the setting of the castor angle, that self-centring ingredient of the steering geometry. A positive increase in this, Lionel explained, should help reduce both the wander and the oversteer.

"Try all that," he said, "and get back to me if none of it helps."

After checking the power-steering box and the steering linkages, most of which had already been replaced, we set about increasing the castor angle. The improvement achieved was certainly noticeable. The general wander was reduced, and the oversteer, which had previously meant backing off the steering as the car progressed through a corner, was now less severe. However, the unpredictable wandering at speed was unchanged.

With no other obvious answers, Lionel ended our next conversation with: "Motor manufacturers face these problems all the time... there are no foolproof formulas. You will just have to keep checking one thing after another... and only make one alteration at a time. Don't confuse the situation by not knowing what particular alteration has caused what change."

All good advice; but, for the life of us, we had no idea where to begin. In desperation, I returned to an old but questionable solution: lead ballast up front. I remember being asked very early on how we might counteract problems with the braking and steering due to the reduction of weight up front. "With lead, if needs be," I had replied. While such an idea might have indeed be good common sense, it might just as easily have been another case, back in university days, of "let's use fencing wire to tie up the timing chain."

If nothing else, it should at least have some sort of deadening effect on the bounce and possibly even help the oversteer. A small drop at the front due to the extra weight would do no harm and the ride height at the rear could easily be matched by altering the setting on the 'level-ride' – the "bicycle pump suspension", as unkindly described by some, with its under-bonnet compressor piping compressed air into bags surrounding the rear shock absorbers.

With Bill's help and that of a local foundry too, the front bumper brackets were enclosed at the top and filled with lead. After which, the bumper was bolted firmly back onto reinforced anchor points on the front of the half-chassis. To my delight, the theory worked: the ride at the front was just right, and the oversteer, although not yet completely cured, was further reduced. So, lead for ballast had not been so silly after all. Furthermore, the Roadster's all-up weight was still several hundred pounds lighter than the standard Seville.

Now what? Well, never mind about the thump at the back, or even  the speed-related wander, which might be due solely to the style of the thirties body. Far more important was the remaining oversteer and the general wandering, both serious obstacles if ever we wanted to produce more of our so-called supercars.

By chance, a technical motor-journalist, on hearing of the Roadster's ailments, offered to "give it the once over", as he put it. When coming face to face, seasoned journalist took to fledgling machine like duck to water, and we all three set off to unravel some seemingly insoluble complexities. Our potential saviour assessed each problem, one by one, heading ever further from our meeting point just to the north of London. Given half a chance, I realised, he would have driven all the way to Birmingham and back.

"Oh, didn't we turn around at that last junction," he murmured in reply to my rather weak but pointed remark of: "Isn't it odd how, when you're driving somewhere on a test run, the journey is only half done when you arrive where you're going!"

When eventually he turned for home, we were more than half an hour into an intended ten-minute drive. Still, who was I to complain? Not only was he enjoying himself but he soon came up with some much-needed answers.

"Has this car got a narrower track at the rear compared to the front, by any chance?" he enquired.

"Yes, I think so," I said, mentally paging through the specifications as best as I could, "but only slightly."

"And have you altered the tyre pressures, front to rear, to take account of the change in weight distribution?" he further asked.

"No," I replied.

As ignorant as such an answer might appear, no one as yet had mentioned tyre pressures in relation to handling. So here was something we had all managed to overlook: Lionel no doubt assuming we had already taken account of so obvious a factor.

When later it came to the unpredictable wandering at higher speeds, our friend put in his all. He was sure it was nothing to do with the Roadster's shape. The almost imperceptible but uncontrolled movement was not something he could recall with other similar-bodied cars. As for the thump at the rear, he seemed quite indifferent either to its consequence or to its cause.

"That's just suspension stuff," he said, while waving his hand at nothing in particular. "There are plenty of specialists in that field... change the shock absorbers or something".

The fact that the Seville's level-ride air-bagged shock absorbers only came in one standard form, and were quite unalterable, was of little interest to our friend. He left, smiling contentedly, promising to give "the wandering" further thought.

Realising that ignorance is only sometimes bliss, the pressure of the rear tyres was set a good few pounds above that of the front; and, by using 'limo' wheel studs supplied by Ohio Bob and special spacers made up by Jack, the rear track was increased to equal that of the front. So, apart from the irritating unpredictable wandering, our newfound rescuer had, virtually at a stroke, transformed the Roadster into effective one-finger steering as we had always hoped.

Suggesting to the others that we sort out the remaining problems over the summer produced instant rebellion. Frank, without so much as a drawn-out rural thought, said I should be satisfied with what we had achieved. Jack, a certain gusto overriding his normal caution, proclaimed "All thirties cars ride and handle badly... and this one is already better than most". Gavin, cheeky smile firmly in place, merely offered: "It's great boss!" and Tom, who was still excited at the Roadster's timely completion, tended towards neutrality. Sandy, needless to say, repeated his relentless eulogies on first seeing the mock-up in the barn: "Anything's possible, anything's possible!" to which, as an afterthought, he threw in: "Wouldn't that policeman who came to the barn change his tune now!"

This apparent flippancy was all very well, but they were not the ones who had asked co-directors and shareholders to finance a prototype for a seemingly sensible and potentially profitable commercial project. In other words, their heads were secure: mine was the one on the block.

Des, to give him his due, made a tentative contribution by suggesting a wind tunnel test. Des, of course, would suggest that: he knew that none of us had the remotest idea how to organise such a test, to say nothing of the likely cost involved. Anyway, our journalist friend had ruled that out. Eventually, Bill, loyal to the end, was the only one who offered to lend a hand.

I then remembered the ex racing and rally driver who I knew through his vintage and classic car parts business back from the days of 158PY. In fact it was he who had eventually tracked down the erstwhile wrong-dipping headlamps. Very early on, when attempting to source the exterior lamps and other special fitments, he had come up trumps.

Items such as old-time door handles, bonnet hinges and catches were easily sourced, as were the side and tail lamps. The headlamps, though, proved much more of a problem. Eventually, in desperation, I had contacted this old acquaintance.

"There's got to be something available in the form of large-diameter rounded headlamps with modern fittings," I had said, having finally tracked him down.

"Well, old boy," he replied, after some thought, "I think I might have the answer. They're American... and could be just what you want. I'll look into it and get back to you."

He was as good as his promise and, when delivered, not only did the pair of gleaming monsters look the part but they were also ideal for mounting on the crossbar between the front wings.

Our old friend, between times buying and selling specialist parts and specialist vehicles, had for years now raced and rallied many an older-style car. He might easily therefore have some answers to our present problems. I telephoned him.

"Would you like to come and see and drive what's attached to your headlamps?" I asked.

"Yes," he said, chuckling, suitably amused at the reversal of importance of the items, "and if I'm given a good meal while doing so, I'll be super-positive towards your machine... as well as to my headlamps of course!"

He was so pleased to have found those headlamps, even if they did dip the wrong way.

"Well," he said, with a relaxed half-smile as he stood looking at the Roadster soon after he had arrived, "it's all right old boy, isn't it? Yes, I like it. But let's take this off," he signalled, patting the roof.

"It doesn't come off," I said.

"What! It has to come off!" he retorted, "It's got to be a convertible, old boy."

"The roof is fixed," I replied. "It can't come off, it's part of the structure. "Anyway, if it did come off, our sporting car wouldn't hold the road properly and it would be noisy too. Come on, drive it and see."

"Got to be a convertible, old boy," he retorted, as I ushered him in through the driver's door, finishing off with, "OK then, let's see, shall we?"

All of six-foot six-inches tall and not exactly slight of build, I could understand why he would have preferred to have the roof off. Still, once settled inside, he perked up, and off we set in search of some deserted country lanes.

After a couple of miles, we turn down a side road. Rounding a corner, we find ourselves at the head of a long, slightly snaking lane. Without the slightest warning, he floors the accelerator. Then, with barely enough time for me to reach for the panic handle, we are hurtling along amid overhanging trees and overflowing wheat. As we continue down the narrow road, with its assorted potholes along the way, I realise he is becoming rather more settled than I care for.

Again without warning, instead of applying the brakes, he sweeps around the almost-blind corner at the end, slows, but only the very barest necessary, and turns down a narrow track into a semi-deserted farmyard. Having performed a full circle sideslip on a not-too-large adjoining concrete slab, he flips the steering the other way, drops a gear and, throttle to the floor once more and engine roaring, leaves through a part-opened gate.

I sat transfixed as he continued his antics, his half-smile seemingly set in stone. Time and again he mumbled the same two things: "Yes, yes, I like it," as he slid around a corner; followed by, as he floored the accelerator, "But where's the other hundred horsepower, old boy?" Then, with another sideslip: "Yes, yes, I like it, but damn it, with all its disc-brakes and limited-slip diff and everything... where's the other hundred horsepower?"

As my brain dulled, and my half-open mouth remained at a loss for words, I decided the best course of action was to emulate my brother-in-law: I clung stoically to the panic-handle and prayed. Back on the main road, he did a quick straight-line sprint, during which he had to admit to enjoying a civilised but, in this instance, very one-sided conversation at speed. Then, to my relief, we were home.

Over lunch, he gave his verdict: "That slight wandering at speed that you are worried about... it's not very noticeable, old boy, and is to be expected of such a car. As to the thump at the back: well, even if you can't change the shocks, the car's still very comfortable. After all, it is only an *occasional* car so I wouldn't be too worried."

He drew breath, and continued: "I have to admit, though, the roof is the exception. The car does corner extremely well and it's certainly very quiet." Then, with one of his more jovial chuckles, he concluded with: "But it would be so much nicer with another hundred horse-power, old boy!"

I declined to answer Old Boy; and, after reminiscing over the steadily collapsing classic car market, he bade farewell and left. While our headlamp friend might not have solved the remaining problems, his undoubted fondness for our one-off beast certainly spurred us on.

Later, reading a magazine article about our 'giver of second opinions', I understood his preoccupation with horsepower. In the article, he claimed still to hold the unofficial London to Edinburgh record, which he had carried out in the middle of the night before the introduction of the general speed limit. Also in the article was the admission that his all-time favourite racer had a massive six hundred horsepower. I was only thankful, therefore, that both car and I had survived and that he considered a mere hundred extra horsepower would suffice.

Lionel was not convinced by our friend's verdict. With the rigidity of the combined monocoque and space-frames, Lionel was sure we could, even within a style from a previous age, achieve *all* the qualities encompassed within the Seville.

"All you can do is continue with that 'tried and tested' method of 'trial and error'," he concluded with his dry, often barely perceptible humour.

I took Bill up on his offer of help. The unpredictable feeling on the steering at medium to higher speeds was at times so slight that we despaired of pinpointing the cause, and I began to realise why Lionel had been so concerned when first he had visited the barn. We, the amateurs, had crudely interfered with some expert engineering of some very clever professionals and were now trying to get to grips with what we, still the amateurs, had no idea how to set about curing.

We backtracked through all we had done. We attempted to evaluate what could be so different with the Roadster compared to the original Seville, other than the outside shape and the weight distribution. In the end, regardless of our efforts, we were unable to throw any light on the steering unpredictability. As for the thump at the rear: until the wandering was cured, we ignored it.

Late one afternoon, while having what we referred to as "one last try", I suddenly felt the erratic movement, more to one side and stronger than normal, almost as though the front end was lifting. It was nothing drastic but discernible all the same. Bill, as the passenger, was less affected; but then, almost together, we noticed the trees alongside the road swaying and swirling furiously in the wind.

The likely answer came to us at once. To my annoyance, someone else had long suspected what we, by chance, had now discovered. If we had followed Des's suggestion and gone in search of a wind tunnel, we would have put the issue to rest at a stroke. It was not the top side that was the problem; it was the underside: there was excessive turbulence, both on the trailing sections of the welded-in front mudguards as well as around the void we had created in front of the engine. The unpredictability was merely caused by the varying strength and direction of the wind.

With the help of the ever-tolerant manager of the sheet-metal works, we under-panelled the lot, all the way from the back of the front mudguards to the tail end of the running boards and, just to be on the safe side, under the back of the rear wings and behind the fuel tank too. The cure was immediate and, as a bonus, the fuel economy improved; as no doubt would the top speed too. Whether Des had been guessing, or he had really thought the issue through, we will never know for sure.

Now, apart from a negligible wander at low speeds, there was only that irritating thump at the rear. Again, more unwarranted help was at hand. A friend of a friend of a friend knew another ex-racing and rallying driver who could literally *feel* a car when put through its paces.

"Why don't you have the car checked out by him?"

"Oh, come on," I said, "he wouldn't want to get involved with a one-off converted Seville. Anyway, we've no budget left for that sort of thing."

"He loves a challenge. Go on, give him a call."

I did, and to my pleasant surprise, he insisted on getting involved without any obligations.

"That's the least I can do. By the sound of what you've been through, you could do with some help. I'm coming to Snetterton Race Track in the next few weeks... that's near you isn't it? Why don't we meet somewhere nearby after work?"

I was sure we had already had more than our fair share of help, but any extra was always welcome. We met up as agreed and brought old Jaws along too, so that he could compare the before and the after. He rather liked the Seville, as a normal road car that is, and got a good feel of what we had started with: a bit soft maybe, but firmer than most American cars and very drivable for over two tons.

Then, having had a good look around the Roadster, including peering along the underside and under the wheel arches, front and back, he ensconced himself comfortably behind the wheel.

Happy with all the controls, he made quietly for the end of the hotel drive. Edging slowly into the road, he aimed the mascot at some distant point ahead, and stopped. I turned to face him: too late. Eyes glazed and jaw stiffened; without warning, his foot went to the floor. This, I realised, was another of those rally-cum-racing drivers who was hell-bent on throwing our creation around the narrow lanes of rural Norfolk and Suffolk. Why, I thought, as the armchair seat pressed me from behind, had I been saddled with two such maniacal hair-raisers in so quick a succession?

On occasions, he attempted to drive sideways and, on others, I could have sworn he was trying to stand the car on its nose. He even tried to see if our cherished machine could take off, land again, continue in the same direction, and stop as he had started.

"Now look at that," he said, as he swung the wheel violently to one side and put both feet hard on the none-too-ineffective power disc brakes. "It shouldn't do that."

What the car was not supposed to do, or why, I was unsure, but the fact that we never ended up in the ditch impressed me no end. As I gathered my composure, I realised that, to whatever he was referring, the car must be capable of better.

"It's not right on such a car," he continued. "You haven't done enough to sort out the weight transfer from front to back. You've tended to concentrate only on the front."

"What do you mean?" I said, more than a little concerned. "Are you implying we have a major problem?"

"Well," he said, "it's not a major problem, but you saw what I've been doing to produce the varying behaviour on different road surfaces. Well, it's a great motorway car... you can't fault that. But the thumping on these undulating roads at the rear, and that lurch just then. It's partly to do with incorrect rear shock absorber damping and partly to do with the spring rate... and you could also do with a stiffer rear anti-roll bar too."

"Are you saying," I said, "that not only can we cure that irritating tail-end thump, but we can also further improve the handling?"

"Yes, of course, once you've synchronised the springs and the shock-absorbers with the weight. It's quite simple really and it would be a shame to leave as it is."

If the solution was so simple, why had none of us worked it out before; me included for that matter? The answer was simplicity itself:

our expert was on another plane. He had made a science of *feeling* cars, often at speeds approaching two hundred miles an hour. When he also mentioned in passing that his grandfather had worked alongside the great Sir Henry Royce, here was yet another case of 'being in the blood'.

Forget the heavier anti-roll bar to assist with super-cornering: the Roadster was not a racing car, and the expense of a one-off bar requiring fourteen bends to fit the Seville's unusual axle arrangement was quite unwarranted. Yet, altering the rear springs and adding an additional pair of shock absorbers alongside the level-rides, eventually cured that thump at the back; and so, at long last, our sporty car had its luxury ride as well.

We eventually even solved the remaining puzzle with the steering. Somehow, for all our checks and re-checks, we had managed to misalign the central position of the varying-ratio steering box. This caused the turn in one direction to have a slightly different ratio to that in the other. In addition, as the centre-point of the steering box is designed to have the least play, there was a tendency to wander in one direction and tighten up in the other. In other words, at a stroke, the *amateurs* had again managed to undo what, over many years, the *professionals* had perfected.

For that, we were not particularly proud; but, with everything finally cured, Bill and I magnanimously forgave the rest of the team for copping out; and they, in turn, forgave us for what they described as "pedantic persistence". Still, everyone was more than pleased with the result, pleased with the knowledge that the Roadster, of which they had all been so much a part, was not just a pretty car after all – it was very much a driver's car too.

Now, with a note of renewed confidence, we could at last involve our car with the outside world. What, though, would the outside world make of what a team of dedicated amateurs had been up to for close on three years? Also, was there any chance that some prospective customers might still queue up to buy some two-ton, two-seat, one-suitcase *toys*?

11. Friendly Acclaim

Now, at last, we could have some fun with the completed machine and possibly indulge in some interesting and amusing dialogue with those we met.

No sooner had I pulled into a filling station on my first long run, than a hand was laid on my shoulder and a friendly voice said: "They don't make them like they used to, do they sir?"

I said nothing, looked rather blank and tried to smile. What was I supposed to say? "No, it's brand new... we've just made it!" Hardly.

What, also, could I say to the person, a little later, who politely said that he never realised cars had electric windows in the nineteen-thirties? Or what about the man who insisted, not so politely, that the Roadster was not in fact a Cadillac, because he knew every thirties Cadillac ever built? He was no better pleased or remotely amused when informed that indeed it was, but not of nineteen-thirties origin.

Being out and about was obviously no way to promote the positive attributes of a limited-edition supercar. Somehow, our attention to old-world classic detail had succeeded in fooling people rather more than intended; and the *fun*, therefore, was short lived. There had to be a better way.

"Well, there are plenty of car shows in the summer," said Jack. "Come to think of it, there are one or two indoor shows a bit earlier. I'll ask around."

A couple of days later, he telephoned to say he had booked the Roadster into the London Classic Car Show at Alexandra Palace, that magnificent multi-acred complex in North London set high up over-looking its own large well-treed park. Jack felt this would go some way to gauging the views of both enthusiasts and collectors alike.

Bill, more cautious, was not so easily convinced: "We should get a bit of a feel for people's reactions before disporting ourselves to a mass of sceptical Londoners," he said; finishing off after a pause, "there'll be thousands of them."

Whether or not we shared Bill's views of ever-sceptical Londoners, we took note of his concern. Also, as he already knew of a suitable local event, and with the rest of us otherwise occupied at the time, we let Bill venture forth to test the water on his own.

"What did they think?" we asked on his return.

"Everyone liked the car very much. They particularly remarked on its condition. There were one or two minor criticisms, though." Then, almost as an afterthought: "One man thought, looking from a distance, that it was an old Delahaye... and everyone thought it was a genuine thirties car."

"Well, what did they say when you told them it wasn't?" a bemused Frank enquired.

"Not much, I don't think they believed me."

"You mean they weren't amused, or interested... or anything?" retorted Frank.

"No, I think they were confused and slightly irritated. One elderly woman... she sounded American... came up and said: 'I surely don't remember Cadillac making a model like this'."

"And what did you say to that?" Jack asked, with a broad grin at the very thought of such a misconception.

"Nothing... what could I?"

"Nothing?" Jack exclaimed.

"No," I interjected, "That's exactly the problem I explained I've been having. We... or at least Gavin... seems to have overdone the authenticity. If we carry on like this, we'll just annoy people."

There was a short silence, after which Jack chipped in: "We ought to make a visual display to go with the car... to help people understand what we've done. Without that, it's very difficult to comprehend."

Before the show at Alexandra Palace, Jack and I selected a range of photographs, each showing a particular stage of the conversion, and stuck them on a portable display; all ready for our allocated spot in the Great Hall, the centrepiece of the main building. At one end of the Great Hall, a dazzling ornate circular stained-glass window filters colour-sprinkled light onto the marbled floor below. Above, running the hall's full length, special internal screening to the glass roof adds a muted glow throughout.

Des, on hearing what we were up to, insisted that he and he alone, on the eve of the show, should transport the car to 'The Palace', as he referred to the grand Victorian splendour. I think he felt that not only did the Roadster have to be delivered in some sort of dramatic style – on the back of his brand new transporter – but he, Himself, had to be there to see the reaction. There being no charge for the privilege, we allowed Des his wish.

Des returned to recount how, on his arrival, he had alighted from the cab and, smiling benevolently to the large and gathering crowd, had proceeded to describe how *he*, and virtually *he* alone, had built the car. In fact, not only did he inform all and sundry of his near daily input, month after month, year after year, but he also explained, in great detail, how he had designed the most intricate of its structural components. What Himself did not admit was that only due to the timely intervention of Himself Senior, who had accompanied him there, was the car not delivered to Wembley Stadium, several miles away, instead.

We forgave Des his excessive fervour – just as a father forgave a son the uncalled-for lapse of attention. We all now realised, where Gavin's pretty body was undoubtedly a visual work of art, that the construction hidden underneath was a structural one. Quite simply, without Des's expertise and his ongoing perseverance, there would have been no Roadster. Furthermore, not only do I doubt that very few others could have achieved what he did, I am quite sure that no one else would have tolerated such constant interference by a bunch of enthusiast engineers.

He was further exonerated when the show opened: everyone, young and old, was more than positive towards our machine, especially now we properly explained everything. Unsuspecting passers-by were spared the embarrassment of: "I remember seeing one when I was a child," or worse still, "My father had one".

Other remarks were more prevalent: "Well, I suppose you think you deserve a medal?" quipped one well-wisher; or: "You all ought to be locked up!" another observed; or even, as one wit ventured: "What are you going to do next... build a spaceship?"

Of all the remarks, though, the most satisfying was when we were referred to as a bunch of "professional amateurs". That, for me at least, meant that I had at last equalled that accolade long-since bestowed on the self-taught seamstress over 158 PY's carpets and headlining – "as professional as the professionals".

Despite all the pleasantries, any number of 'Bill's Londoners', very firmly but very politely, commented on almost every visible imperfection: all those details in both design and finish that we had hoped would go unnoticed. So, if we were serious about making more of something that, by its very nature, would always be expensive, we would have to cure every last imperfection.

Most of them were small and inexpensive to rectify, but time-consuming all the same. Accordingly, when time allowed, we shuffled our now part-acclaimed creation from one professional amateur to the other, curing the defects, one by one. By the time of the next show, a major two-day open-air event on a disused airfield, the only corrective work left undone was the not-quite-perfect state of the engine compartment and a couple of design faults in the forward section of the front wings.

The engine compartment, we concluded – with Sandy's blissful agreement and a reluctant nod from Des – was for *propelling* the car and only needed to be neat and tidy. The design faults in the front wings, on the other hand, would have to cede to common sense. By now, the total hours spent to convert original sedan into ultimate Roadster were nearly three times those initially allocated. Due only to the vast majority of these having been done for the sheer challenge, or at a greatly reduced rate, was our first-off budget not greatly overspent. Furthermore, if everything else was cured, we believed that the design faults would fade into obscurity.

Then, without warning, a London City banker contacted us. This friendly financier had heard about the Roadster and felt sure we should be able to make more: and at a profit too.

Having arranged a date and time, we met up at our North London factory on a bright spring day. After a thorough inspection of offices, works and anything else that took an inquisitive banker's fancy, we headed north into the countryside, with me at the wheel. We reached a suitable spot in a lay-by on a good open road and swapped places.

Very gently, he pulled out onto the dual carriageway, keeping well to the inside lane. Now he speeds up a bit, not too much, and a beam spreads across his face. He is obviously enjoying himself immensely. He speeds up some more and the beam changes to a contented smile. He half turns, no doubt to impart some note or judgement: something catches his eye. Wide-eyed, he looks past me, his jaw dropping.

I swing my head to the right: too late. Wallop! Scscscr! Thump! I, too, stare in disbelief. There, up against, and almost attached to the Roadster, wobbling uncontrollably and destroying the side of a beautiful dark blue right front wing, is a not-insubstantial delivery van: a proverbial white one at that. There had been no real feeling of the impact, only the noise of twisting, scraping aluminium: the solid mass of Lionel's "battering-ram" space-frame below just continued, uninterrupted, on its way.

I glance back to my left. There, dissolving into a combination of confused apology and erupting anger is the friendly banker.

"Don't worry," I say, as his incoherent mumbling rises to a peak, "keep calm..." then remembering Paul's statement on first setting eyes on our part-finished machine, add: "It's only a car, it's only a bit of metal." There is no reply. There is still no reply when I add the calming news: "The van's not stopping but I've got its registration number," and rattle it off several times.

He slows and pulls to a halt; we each open our respective doors and jump out. Instead of coming round to inspect the damage, he continues mumbling on the other side of the car. As he persists with his dissertation, I look more closely – then do a double take. In those early days of mobile telephones, our friendly banker, while speaking in a suitable legal monotone, is issuing an 'all points bulletin' to the local police.

"What are you doing?" I asked, partly in disbelief and partly in awe, "We've got his number. He could be anywhere by now."

"It's got to be done," was his curt reply. "We can't have that sort of thing going on."

How he thought the police were going to catch the culprit now, when he must already be well away, I had no idea. As always, to settle our shattered nerves, we made for the nearest pub. We parked a battered car and headed off to ensconce ourselves comfortably inside. There, while I contemplated an embarrassed return to the office with a partly disfigured company asset, our friend bemoaned a banker's fate worse than death: of being personally responsible for devaluing a potentially profitable investment.

No more than ten minutes into our mutual commiseration, a bleeping from deep within his pocket jolts us back to reality. To his satisfaction and to my astonishment, we are summoned to identify the cause of our gloom. Arriving at the scene to smiles and handshakes all around, we are asked to make our inspection. We quickly match the unusual blue on the all-white panels and say: "Yes officer, that's the one." While such a turnaround might not have been an instant cure for our damaged car, it certainly proved most satisfying.

Yet what about the two-day show, now only a week away? How could we evaluate the reactions to our now tidied up machine with an annihilated front wing? In fact, how could we put the car in the show at all?

"Throw a blanket over it," said Bill, when he saw the result of our altercation, his laid-back manner coming fully to the fore.

"What do you mean 'throw a blanket over it'?" Jack said, staring at him as though he had finally slipped over the edge.

"Well, the organiser's have asked for both the before and the after... the standard Seville and the Seville Roadster. So, if you park the two cars side by side, so that the damaged wing is on the inside next to the Seville, you can 'throw a blanket over it'."

We were speechless. Still, Bill was right. When the time came for the cars to be ushered into their smartly roped-off patch, we settled in with our display of photographs and other explanations, and put a large neutrally coloured dustsheet over the damaged wing. On top of the dustsheet, we scattered a few documents and assorted brochures, which, to the unaccustomed eye, appeared as though the Roadster's wing was deliberately being used as a table.

We had a full contingent: Gavin was there, having swapped his overalls for smart attire and a brand-new trilby, as were rural Frank, precision Jack and laid-back Bill, to say nothing of mechanical expert Tom. Our daughter had joined in with several of her now less marauding friends, as had my father-in-law too. Situated next to the main arena, we were all very comfortable with deck chairs and picnic, complete with our own mini-bar in Jaw's plush North American trunk.

Hour after hour, we explained anything and everything to all who enquired. We had the normal questions of "how" and "why" and did our best to be as rational with our answers as we could.

Then, unannounced, a show-ground official appears doing a live commentary over a mobile public address system.

"What's this then?" he asks, partly screwing up his face, as he stops in front of the Roadster.

"Oh, it's just one of those," I reply, pointing to Jaws, while trying to distract his gaze from the blanket; after which I add: "*slightly modified.*"

Even as I uttered the words, I realised it was hardly the most intelligent thing to have said.

"Oh yes. So what exactly have you *modified*?" he asks, thrusting the microphone towards me.

I did my best to explain, as concisely and as accurately as possible, while he, barely inches from my face, retained a fixed, forced smile. No sooner had I finished, than he removed the microphone and having, by the look on his face, believed little of what I had said, continued with: "Well, you all heard that." This was followed by, as an aside, but still into the microphone: "And I wonder how it *drives* after all that *cutting up*?" With which, he forced a grin in my direction and, vigorously chesting the microphone, made clear there would be no 'right of reply'.

As he made off in search of his next victim, that, I thought, would be of no help to further production prospects for our car. It should, however, teach me to be less flippant in future when talking to roving commentators: with or without microphones.

While still recovering from the ordeal, I started to notice several potential enquirers glancing fleetingly in the direction of Jaws. I looked to see what was so interesting about the before, rather than the after. There, sitting in the front were two familiar figures. That in itself might have been all right; but, in this instance, they were quite oblivious of the lookers-on round about. If not for the soundproof nature of modern cars, at least one snore would, I am sure, have been heard either from my father-in-law or his beloved daughter. The Back-up and her father, it appeared, had gone on strike.

I advanced on the car and, to the general mirth of all around, and for some reason to Gavin in particular, very quietly opened the door and, in a deliberately forced whisper, announced: "Do you mind not sleeping in the exhibits," followed up with, somewhat facetiously, "you might *frighten* the customers."

They awoke with a start and, innocent to the last, claimed to have seen all the attractions at least twice, the one professing a normal pref-erence for horses and the other for aeroplanes. With neither of their preferences present at the show, they declined to come the following day.

By the end of the show, despite roving reporters and sleeping beauties, everyone who visited over the two days seemed to like what we had done; except, that is, yet again, the design faults on the forward section of the visible undamaged front wing.

When, a short time later, we came to sort out the repair on the damaged wing, Des was particularly pushy about curing the design faults in *both* wings.

"Considering the trouble you gave us to get the *colour* right, you could at least try and get the *shape* right, now couldn't you? " he declared, with one of his more scolding looks, "So dip your hand in your tight pocket, and have the other wing sorted out as well... then I'll paint them both at cost."

The "tight pocket" was a little unkind, but it was true about the colour. Back then, Jack had come across an old motoring calendar with a regal two-tone blue Duesenberg, that all-time thirties American classic, adorning the month of May. The decision had been instant: all we needed was to match the colours, so off I went to see Des.

"Des," I called out, as he had disappeared across the body-shop, no doubt hurrying away at the sight of my approach. Catching up, I held out the calendar: "How do we create these colours?" I had asked, "Would they be standard by any chance?"

"I wouldn't have thought so," he replied, barely looking up from what he was doing. "They don't keep colours for fifty years or more...

and that's not a very standard sort of colour, or a standard sort of car for that matter."

"Well, there can't be that many variations of blue. Surely you can find something to match?"

"I think there are about thirty thousand 'standard' colours to date and none of them look like the ones on that car," he replied coldly.

"Thirty thousand colours!" I exclaimed.

"Yes," he replied, "Colours are very complex. We go on courses to learn about them, you know. There are over ninety base colours to mix from, so you can imagine how many variations that can produce."

I had again stepped in way over my head, and without Jack or Bill for support. I remembered years earlier there being no difficulty sourcing a colour when having a car re-sprayed. On reflection, on that occasion, I had requested something standard straight off the shelf.

"Des," I said, with concern, "couldn't you match the colours by mixing them yourself?"

"I wouldn't want to try, and certainly not from a photograph," he replied, then adding almost as an afterthought: "I know someone who might, though."

After a further lecture on the intricacies of his trade, I was given the name and telephone number of his paint supplier.

"From a printed photograph in a calendar?" the paint supplier half-said and half-enquired. "That won't be easy. There are so many highlights on a photograph. How will you know exactly which shade or tone you want?"

Over the next two months, after as many trials in as many weeks on little square test cards, we ended up with a complex mixture of seven base colours for one of the blues and five for the other. Was it worth the trouble? Well, as the final two blues received unanimous approval from both team and helpers alike and the last-but-one samples were almost unanimously rejected, that must surely speak for itself. Des, as so often, had been right; and Jack and I were only too glad that it had only taken two months to sort out.

That was then: now we were having to make a decision over the banker's battered wing together with its mate on the other side. I consulted the Young Professor to see what he had to say.

"Des is right," said Gavin, "we can't possibly re-build the right-hand wing leaving the faults as they are. Get him to strip the paint off both wings and I'll sort out the left-hand one while I'm remaking the right... and you can buy me a really good meal... plenty of good wine and all."

What could I say? As always, not a lot, other than: "Yes please... thank you."

So the friendly banker's undeserved mishap produced an unexpected bonus after all. Still, when the time came to do the work, Des uncovered an added problem: "Where," he asked, "are the instructions for removing the wings?"

"There aren't any," was the answer.

So, being the only one at the time available with the detail knowledge, I was handed some overalls and, insurance job or not, told to help. How we forgot the instructions, I have no idea. I remember, at a very early age, being informed of the importance of the paperwork. I can still see that notice, stuck to the back of the door of the 'little boys room' in an old country hotel nestling amongst those undulating Southern African hills: "The job's not done till the paperwork's finished!"

The *paperwork*, on this occasion several thousand words of do's and don'ts together with a set of full-colour modified wiring diagrams, was eventually *finished* and the *job* finally *done*.

When the repairs and the wing modifications were complete, Frank invited us to join a gathering of classic cars at a rural fund-raiser. The Roadster would be welcome, he said, alongside the many others of all ages and types on display. Having still not completely given up on further production – if the ever-continuing recession should eventually end – any reactions would be welcome, especially with the front wings now fully cured.

"Yes," I replied, "but I'll ask Bill to bring it along as I'll be away at the time."

I duly contacted Bill. He was free and happily agreed to join up with Frank for the day.

When I returned after the event, there in the garage, placed squarely on top of the Roadster, was a great victory trophy. A note attached from Bill explained that our now fully completed car had been awarded second prize in the judging on the day. I telephoned him instantly.

"What's this all about," I asked. "What was the competition... and who was first?"

"There were prizes for the three best cars," explained Bill, "all judged by popular public vote," After which, almost as an aside, he added, "Frank was first."

"Frank was first... The farmer beat us?" I exclaimed, natural rivalry coming to the fore.

"Yes, but it's not all that bad... we also beat him."

"What do you mean?" I asked, a trifle confused.

"Well," he continued, "it wasn't his favourite car that won. His favourite car was third. So you see, you both won really."

If not for having been judged by members of the public, one might have suspected the result had been rigged. Out of all the cars, one of Frank's classics along with his more modern super-sports-car and the Roadster had been chosen as the top three. That had to be a true accolade for the Roadster, proving that at last it was truly finished.

Thus, a concerned team leader, with the last-minute help of a slow-driving friendly banker, appeared to have been competent after all. Despite that, as time progressed, neither the friendly bankers nor the professional amateurs were able to contrive a way of producing more, or certainly not at a semblance of an economical price in the prevailing conditions. So, barring a major change in the economic outlook, we would have to accept that there would be no sudden production run of exotic machines, whether off our or anyone else's manufacturing line. Therefore, for the time being at least, the tenth-scale plans, the multitude of notes, the scratchy sketches and the templates were filed under 'on hold'.

As for the team, without whom not a bolt, not a screw or even the smallest piece of upholstery would have been undone, let alone put back together again, with the late-eighties boom settling into the early-nineties recession, they would have to succumb to the added pressures this produced, as did we all.

So too would everything have to succumb, just as would our one-off machine. Despite not having cost that much in cash terms, some sort of commercial use would have to be found for a seemingly redundant prototype.

12. Use Or Abuse?

Regular everyday use of the Roadster continued to prove as questionable as ever. A fellow shopper at a local supermarket, having enquired and been told of the trials and tribulations involved in the car's making, simply remarked: "Oh, didn't you know you could buy ready-made cars in showrooms these days?"

An elderly family friend, on hearing the same sagas, reacted slightly differently: "But, my dear, considering the trouble you've been through... and with only two seats and using so much fuel, why did you ever make such a car? Was it a mistake?"

The answer to the first question has to be "yes", and to the second, hopefully, "no". Yet, both tend to indicate that the measure of common sense involved in the project's undertaking was not much greater than that displayed during earlier schemes in Africa.

Reactions of the younger generation had changed little. A rather more mature marauding teenager, lounging comfortably viewing a stretched-out bonnet through a narrow slit windscreen, eagerly announced: "It's really *cool*... just like a truck."

"Like a truck!" I exclaimed in disbelief.

Despairing of such remarks, or of ever finding suitable gainful employment for our machine, I contacted a couple of our European distributors to see if they had any ideas.

"Would you," our agent in France asked, "be prepared to bring the car to a sales conference in Paris... a sort of PR exercise for your company, and something different for our staff?"

Here then was a possibility after all: a corporate PR tool. Others in the company were not so sure: "You're not proposing to *drive* it all the way to Paris, are you?"

"Why not?" I retorted.

"It might break down... or get damaged. Anything might happen."

"Come on," I replied, "it's a car and it needs to be used. There's no more reason for it to break down or to be damaged, whether in France or anywhere else. We can hardly leave it permanently locked up in a garage... now can we?"

Good sense, of one kind or another, did eventually prevail and two of us set off for Paris. We boarded the cross-channel ferry, happy in the knowledge that the Roadster was finally earning its keep. No sooner had we reached Calais, than a group of regal-red Ferraris, waiting to board the ferry, spotted the two-tone blue modified Seville disembarking.

"What's that car?" we could see them saying as they peered in our direction. Then, as one of them came to investigate, our queue moved off; but not before, with eyebrows suitably raised, he trumpeted the marque back to his friends for all around to hear. We smiled and, suitably encouraged, headed on our way: we had left our mark with the best.

We reached Paris well on time, attended the conference, completed our tour and returned home; and not a beat was missed. We even circumnavigated the Arc de Triomphe in the rush hour and ventured onto the Périphériqe; and, despite some gesticulations and the occasional wave, never received so much as a proverbial scratch. A point had been made, and the Roadster had begun to earn its keep.

That, though, was short lived. As the early-nineties recession deepened further and the ensuing war in the Gulf brought industry almost to a halt, requests for goodwill visits ceased. All we could now do was attend shows and other functions, ever hopeful that something might turn up.

My father-in-law, with his unequivocal love of aeroplanes, agreed to accompany me to a Tiger Moth rally at Woburn Abbey. The show seemed as good an opportunity as any to push the Roadster to the fore, especially as its style emanated from a similar era to that of the aeroplanes.

As we passed through the imposing ornate wrought-iron gates, we were greeted with waves and smiles from all around. We were quickly ushered past queues of waiting cars and through the pay-booths, without the slightest suggestion of our having to pay. The marshals, authority established by their brightly coloured armbands, majestically cleared a way for us between the eager, gesticulating crowds, directing us finally to the very forefront of the aerial display.

No sooner were we parked than members of the public rushed upon us, bombarding us with questions, to all of which we had no answers: "You're early, aren't you... we weren't expecting you for another half hour?" and, "Aren't you supposed to be on that side of the rope over there?" or, "I can't see you on the programme... what was it in?"

Either the Roadster had somehow been acclaimed without our knowledge, and nationally at that, or we were being mixed up with someone else. Our only responses took the form of polite smiles intermingled with suitably confused, if inane stares.

Finally, when Chitty Chitty Bang Bang turned up, along with others of similar note, we discovered this was 'Woburn Day' of the Great British Film Rally, staged to promote British Films and Television and raise money for Save the Children. Not only had all the participants been allocated a prime position at the air display, but they were also entitled to free entry to the park.

The owner of Chitty Chitty Bang Bang, who to the children's delight acted out Oliver Hardy antics, insisted that we park alongside. When I protested that the Roadster had never been near a film, let alone *in* one, all he said was: "Well, it looks as though it should have... so please join us."

A compliment indeed and endless possibilities of gainful employment entered a furtive mind. Hearing also that the incident was to be written up by 'Our Man at The Standard', London's long-time daily newspaper's motoring correspondent, possibilities of stardom and international success rushed in too.

When the article appeared as the week's lead item in the motoring section, everything for which we could have hoped was there: pictures of the before and of the after, explanations of what had been done in its making and even a description of how the stylish machine was 'aimed' by its mascot way out front. That said, I could have brained 'Our Man' for the headline: "History in the Faking"

Such a label was hardly likely to help our motorcar find employment in films, television or anything else. Yet, to give 'Our Man' – or his editor – his due, he was not far off the mark really: Gavin's flowing curves were a tribute to their time and had, as we already knew, confused many already. Anyway, as the Roadster's roof is permanently attached to its body, I somehow doubt our brush with the entertainment world would have come to much. That statement of old, when discussing whether our 'sports-car that never was' at university should have a roof or not, raised its head again: "How would anyone see who was inside?"

Still, if nothing else, our insisting on that mascot being "way out front" had been worth the battle. Jack had nearly had a seizure when asked to machine the lightly cast Seville emblem to fit into a drilled-out Rolls-Royce radiator cap.

"Drilling through a chromed brass radiator cap is one thing, but how am I supposed to machine *this*?" he had said, holding up the wreath and crest emblem. "How do you suggest I secure a fancy enamelled casting like this in a lathe?"

As he received no reply – because there was none – he mumbled to himself, shook his head and walked off. Being Jack, and knowing how much we wanted that mascot to sit proudly out front – just as the flying-lady had on 158PY and the winged B had on Bruce's Bentley – he somehow succeeded. When done, not a mark or a scratch was to be seen. Asked how, he just smiled and responded: "Tricks of the trade!" Some tricks, some trade, we thought, and questioned him no further.

For all the disappointment of nothing coming of being mistaken for a film car, one other problem cropped up with irritating regularity that hindered the Roadster's intended productive future: its drivability. Just as the roving reporter at the open-air show had claimed, "I wonder how it *drives* after all that *cutting up*?" so the accusation of, "Without proper 'on track' tests, the Roadster will likely display any number of unforeseen weaknesses," was a suggestion we had heard rather too often now.

An old family friend, and one of the dismissive sceptics at the project's outset, suggested we permanently counter such insinuations by having the car tested on a reputable racetrack. Algenon, or Algi as we all knew him, having headed into the banking world at a very early age, bore little similarity to the friendly banker who had disfigured the Roadster's wing. A cynic at the best of times, Algi tended to call a spade a shovel and, if so inclined, with sharp teeth on.

In fact, when first we had admitted outside our small collective band to the Roadster's existence, not only did Algi ask some very awkward questions but, to my concern, he also expressed an interest in seeing what we had been up to. Considering the likely reaction to what we had so far done, I had thought it best to warn Bill of his impending visit to the barn.

"Oh, I would enjoy meeting him," Bill had said, rubbing his chin and contemplating another roll-up, "he's well known in the Morgan Club. He was one of the early club members to be involved in racing. I think I have an article about him somewhere... I'll try to find it."

"I didn't know Algi was involved in racing Morgans," I said with some astonishment, but at the time gave the surprise revelation no further thought. We had enough on our minds back then working out how to modify two de-skinned Seville rear doors to fit a much narrower style of body.

Bill, true to his word, the very next day produced an old back-issue of the Morgan Club magazine. He turned to a picture on the inside rear cover of some Team Morgan racers of twenty or so years earlier.

"There," he said, pointing to one of them, "that's him."

I looked; and I looked again. Standing beside one of the Morgans, with race number emblazoned on its side, was a young man with hair down to his shoulders. No, not the clean-shaven banker in the neat city suit, surely not? Yes it was: Algi's name was clearly printed underneath. How extraordinary, I thought; and what with Bill still having this old publication.

"Can I borrow it?" I asked, as the implication of the unearthed find sunk in. "Yes," replied Bill with a smile, and I was presented with the magazine on the spot.

I invited Algi to stay with us the night before his visit. Then, over an early-evening drink, as he launched forth on some complex financial theory, I casually handed him the magazine.

"You didn't tell me you were involved in racing Morgans," I said, pointing to the picture.

He tried, with some reasonable success, to hide his surprise at the reappearance of this best-forgotten piece of history – as well as his concern as to whose hands it now was in.

"Oh, yes, that is me, isn't it? Yes, I did have longer hair then, didn't I," he replied, his tone a touch subdued. At which, with a change of subject that would have done a magician's sleight of hand proud, the discussion ended as quickly as it had begun.

The next morning, when first confronted with our metallic creation, Algi made some polite but meaningless comments. Then, having introduced Bill, his interest veered politely towards "how we were going to do this", or "why were we doing that". The magazine was undoubtedly having the desired effect: none of his 'fanged shovels' had yet appeared.

"What seems to be the problem here?" he asked, looking at the partly cut-up, partly fitted door with its lock mechanism protruding well beyond the extremities of a sleek thirties-style car.

"Oh, the door locks are a bit wide," I answered, trying to hide the ongoing concern over this perplexity that had baffled Bill and I for days. We knew we would end up with countless problems with the closing and locking and the internal workings of the doors if we were unable to use the original locks.

While carrying on an animated Morgan dialogue with Bill, Algi stopped at one of the partly disassembled, discarded original Seville front doors. He peered inside, felt around at some bit or other on its extreme edge and reappeared again to check the outside. He looked up, eyebrows raised.

"Why not use *these* locks instead?" he said. "They seem more like what you need."

In the end, much to our surprise, this simple observation saved days of work, to say nothing of the many sleepless nights too. Having assumed in this age of super mass-production that the front and rear locks would be the same, we had not even bothered to check – in fact, they could hardly have been more different. So, Algi's eventual half-hour, with its near continuous double-sided Morgan banter, was both sane and useful, but in strict contrast to what was written on the sceptical banker's face when first entering the barn. If not for that old club magazine, I suspect there would have been a string of comments ranging anywhere from: "Does it run on elastic bands?" to, "This time, you really must have fallen off a mental precipice!"

Now, several years later, was Algi again offering sound rational advice by suggesting we put our one-of-a-kind on the track; or was he perhaps trying to get his own back for my having kept that magazine? For my part, there was understandable concern: could we really put our hard-toiled, one-and-only Roadster to such a test? Such thoughts were further fuelled by memories of the University Buick running its big end while attempting a similar ploy on a local race circuit in Africa all those years ago.

As for the team, Tom, while sure that his magnificent power-plant would endure such extremes, was only really concerned for the pristine blue paint nearest the exhaust. Frank, who between growing crops and rearing turkeys had for years been a keen motor racer, was really quite supportive; and young Gavin, who had recently acquired a sporty Ford Escort XR3, merely exclaimed with one of his typical grins: "Go on Boss, give it a whirl?"

On the other hand, Bill, knowing the normal antics of his racing customers, thought the plan might be, as he put it, "a trifle risky." Jack was genuinely concerned and Sandy, for the only time I can remember, attested to a real fear for his now described "magnificent beast". Des, though, was almost apoplectic, and made quite clear that he would not be carrying out any more repairs at cost.

Despite these reservations, we arranged to join a small group at Goodwood, that world-famous circuit of the nineteen-forties, fifties and sixties, and reputed to be one of the fastest unbanked tracks still in use. One of their expert drivers would take control and confirm or deny what others had expounded in private, possibly expanding on their findings. Certainly, if we were ever in a position to make more of our exotic machines, such an exercise would be the ultimate test of structure and fittings.

None of the team being available on the allotted day, I took along our now ten-year-old son on this novel and potentially exciting experience. We set off together on a perfect dry, windless day, skirting London, then heading south to weave our way through the picturesque Sussex countryside towards the coast.

We arrived on time and drove through the narrow entrance tunnel under the track to arrive at the pits. Prior to the now famous Goodwood Revival Meetings, the start of the two-and-half mile track was bounded on the inside by the somewhat archaic pits and, on the outside, by a large open lawn running up to a particularly tired-looking tearoom and restaurant. The remainder of the track, encircling the training and testing facilities and the aerodrome, was bounded by grassland and trees. The stands had long since been removed when the glory days had ended. As a counter to the sense of overall neglect, high above, on a hill overlooking the circuit, was 'Glorious Goodwood', with its pinnacled multi-domed grandstand silhouetted on the skyline, sitting waiting for racers of the four-legged kind.

We parked up next to several highly tuned Jaguars, Porsches and even a Ferrari or two. Bliss for someone who had once thought his father had ruined a perfectly good Seville. Now, at the sight of such a throng, he at last appeared won over, convinced that no normal Seville would have been invited to join this lot.

Having teamed up with our nominated professional driver, I was informed that, provided the car proved itself competent, I would be allowed on the track for a circuit or two on my own. At this, Dad was more than exonerated: Dad was about to become a budding race driver. Not so: little did son realise that Dad was long past his sell-by date as far as this sport was concerned.

What about the Roadster, though? Did it let itself, or any of the team, down? It most certainly did not. In the professional's capable hands, our concoction – as Adolf had so described it – fair flew along those straights and, despite the screaming of the tyres piercing the innermost depths of an ultra-soundproofed cab, fair swept around the corners too. The clockwise track forced me towards the inside; then, at the left-right corner on the back straight and again at the chicane near the start, I was thrown firmly back against the door. No ordinary seat belts could restrain such sideways force and, as always, my only saviour was the panic-handle fixed solidly above the door.

Lap after lap we thundered down those straights, each time faster than the last. Each time, as a corner came into view, my eyes and brain told me "we're off the track"; but no, as the screaming resumed and my body lifted sideways, muscles strained, around we went, not a creak or a groan. Time and again repeated and, time and again, a voice from within shouted that we were doomed. Yet, not a wobble, not a flicker, just a lurch from left to right and back again, twice each time around. This was no desert-defying Oldsmobile or highland-cornering Seville: this low-slung bit of *foreign* metal was keeping up with some very eminent machinery indeed.

Our valiant tester-of-the-unknown particularly liked the progressive braking and, surprisingly for a racing fanatic, the great big leather armchair seats too. He did not, however, much care for the column gear change or the truck-like visibility. Despite the stresses, nothing broke and nothing came adrift. Our racy Roadster did, though, fail its race-track 'heat test'. This entailed completing two laps in second gear with the accelerator held firmly to the floor reaching speeds approaching a hundred miles an hour. Quite understandably, as far as my simple reasoning went, the engine boiled.

Nevertheless, our advisor tracked down the problem merely to the lack of a fan shroud. GM had very sensibly supplied a more than adequate two-piece shroud but we, in our unfailing wisdom, had reasoned that the Roadster could do without it. I suppose it could have, if nobody rushed around in second gear at nearly a hundred miles an hour – or drove through Death Valley for that matter. Perish either thought: this one occasion was quite enough and, thankfully, our car had survived.

All the same, we should never have left off the fan shroud, and would now somehow have to squeeze it in. That, along with our test driver's suggestion of doubling-up the rear anti-roll bar instead of changing the existing one, would make useful winter distractions. The additional bar, as he pointed out, would both improve the cornering while also reducing the excessive noise from the leading front tyre.

What about that accusation by our old racing and rallying friend of headlamp fame: "Where's the other hundred horsepower?" On that score, another fifty or so would do nicely; but as the old 5.7 litre lean-burn engine ran on unleaded fuel and still passed its emission tests, we felt at least these qualities should remain: then our creation could be considered reasonably 'green' as well.

Despite the positive nature of it all, my emotions were not quite in tune with those of our son. Yes, of course I felt a sense of exhilaration and pride, but tinged with a feeling of mild terror for the well being of

our machine. We had undoubtedly confirmed the Roadster's c
ity and even some raceability, as well as establishing that the be
the seventies – *slightly* modified – measured up more than favourab
to the nineties.

That said, we were still no nearer finding an occupation for our
unemployed machine. Without the crowds that had flocked to see
Stirling Moss and others, some thirty years earlier, we were hardly
likely even to rate mention in the local village publication. We
certainly gained the animated support of those others involved in the
day's event. Yet, when we met up afterwards, there were still no ideas,
only questions.

When asked why more of our exotic cars were not being made, I
hastily explained the time-consuming complexities involved, to say
nothing of the present state of the classic car market. Furthermore,
without it being a first-time challenge and without a potential pot of
gold at the end, we would certainly not be making any more the way
we made this one.

At which, some bright spark pipes up: "Well, if you really want to
do something different, why not see if you can undo what you've done
and put it all back the way it was? Now, that would be a real
challenge!"

When the laughter had subsided and the culprit almost thrown
from his chair, I decided, for the first time, outside family and close
friends, to tell stories of corrugated iron box-carts and university cars
that never were. When finished, the silence was only broken by: "Well,
it was third time lucky... perhaps you'd better not chance a fourth!"

When we arrived home, not quite to a hero's welcome, I was at
least forgiven my apparent lapse of sanity. I even had the feeling, when
telling stories of "sweeping round here" and "thundering down there",
that some of the team were just a little more pleased than prepared to
let on: the professionals had given the amateurs the thumbs up; the
doubters had conclusively been countered.

Still, had any of us at the outset realised what would be involved in
the Roadster's design, its engineering and its one-off making, and
especially had we known that the value of classic cars would plummet
no sooner had we finished, we would never have contemplated such a
scheme – let alone started it.

In the end, as the recession deepened rather than turning, the great

head scratching, and regardless of the artistic and
, could no more conjure up a worthwhile commer-
e-off creation than they had been able to work out
to make more. The only thing now, I thought, was
of how stupid we had been to believe, as non-
nals, that we could achieve commercial success
with something akin to an extended DIY project. Nobody could then
accuse us of having not made every logical – and likely illogical – effort
to maximise our ill-fated Roadster's potential.

So, as I put pen to paper, and as company finances becoming ever
more stretched, we knew, without some chance use being found or
some lucky orders received by the company – and in a hurry too – that
our cherished machine would have to go.

13. Out Of The Blue

Only by everyone putting in an enormous effort – and with the support of long-term loyal customers – was the Roadster not found a good home. Later, with the dousing of the Kuwait oil-well fires, the world economic gloom lifted and the redundant prototype returned to its PR role.

Then, in an attempt to clarify the implications of putting on paper all that we had done, especially to someone else's corporate product, I made another of those uninvited telephone calls to Detroit.

"No, there can be no objection to you using our trade names in a book providing of course your story is true," the voice replied, at the same time suggesting from what I described that I also contact Public Relations. This I did, to which I was told to send photographs and brief explanation; this I also did.

"I love it," an American voice echoed down the telephone barely a week later. "If you don't bring that car here, I'm flying over to have a ride in it! How did you do that to a '78 Seville? It's not possible. Tell me more?"

Having long since accepted the Roadster's relegation to ultimate obscurity, here was a far-away voice, that of a senior motor industry executive, getting mightily excited about our questionable enterprise from several years past. A sudden re-awakening welled up inside.

"Yes, of course it would be fantastic if the car visited the States sometime," I replied. How or when, I dared not think.

"Leave it with me," said the voice, and the conversation ended as abruptly as it had started.

Several weeks later, a woman's soft, gentle American voice came on the line: "Is that the owner of the converted Seville?"

"Well, the 'keeper' of," I replied. "How can I help?"

"The Cadillac Division of General Motors has asked me to interview you about it," she said.

With memories of roving commentators and headline-writing editors, I was at first hesitant. Still, as the questioning continued, I relaxed and expanded on how and why the team had done what they had. The interview ended with the assurance that we would hear more.

As the weeks passed, I thought, and with good reason, that GM USA, when dealing with old-world enthusiasts, had decided discretion was the better part of valour.

Not so: one morning several months later, a hefty bundle with a Detroit postmark came tumbling through the letterbox. Inside were several of the same issue of a monthly publication, 'Cadillac Voice'. I unfolded one and looked through, page-by-page, article-by-article. There was plenty about new models, but nothing about some Englishmen having cut up and re-shaped one of their more celebrated older models.

I reached the back page; and did a double take. Covering the top third of the page was a photograph of the Roadster larger than any other picture in the publication and, below, covering another third of a page, was the article.

No sooner had copies been run off and sent to each of the team, than the town's local newspaper wanted the story too. When that appeared, the editor had taken it upon himself to adopt the Roadster as the standard-bearer of the town's manufacturing expertise. Several weeks later, at an outing with our two local Classic Car Clubs, we were approached by a freelance journalist who suggested a full-length feature for a national magazine.

"Yes," we agreed, Bill hastily adding: "But you must drive the car and comment on its handling... it wasn't built just to be looked at you know!"

"Certainly," the ever-eager journalist replied, with a glint in his eye.

By now, the radiator shroud and the rear anti-roll bar had long since been fitted, and to good effect too, and the interview, inspection and road test went off without a hitch. The article, when published, contained praise for the Roadster's style, comfort, handling and even the exotic extras – everything, except for those fifty missing horses. This time, the reference to "a sheep in wolf's clothing" did not go down well with the team: the very heart of their creation had been criticised, and for all to see.

Luck, as so often, was at hand, this time in the form of a telephone call from 'Buffalo Bill': "You remember some time ago," the gruff voice said, "one of you asked if I had a bigger matching engine to fit that sports machine you lot made. Well, I've found one that I didn't know I had. I don't know what it's like inside, but it seems to turn over by hand all right."

Buffalo Bill was the long-time owner of several acres of redundant foreign metal alongside Heathrow Airport who, over the years, had helped with any number of emergencies. At times, he produced some vital mechanical component, at others, something to cure the result of a brush with a gatepost and, at still others, some piece of the interior to rectify the result of a badly aimed cigarette.

"How much do you want for the engine?" Tom asked, as he contemplated the possible interpretation of "seems to turn over all right".

"To you lot," he replied, after some thought – and not being one to deny himself the luxuries of life – "how about... let's say... the equivalent of a case of Scotch?"

Tom was amazed. At that price, worn-out or otherwise, this represented barely the price of a new cylinder head, let alone a whole gigantic 6.6 litre interchangeable engine. After taking delivery, Tom, excitement rising at the very prospect, set about doing another of his dismantle-check-and-cleans; on yet another *magnificent* engine. When opened, there, to everyone's astonishment, were the barely worn innards of a perfectly preserved late-seventies' power plant.

"That engine you sold us," Tom said, having contacted our benefactor, "it's almost brand new. You virtually *gave* it to us."

"Good on you... I like your car!" was followed by a raucous laugh; and that was all he had for a reply. Yet again, what could any of us say?

Now, in order to retain the Seville's electronic fuel injection while also increasing the compression, Tom re-used the smaller bored 'top end' from the original engine; and the ever-tolerant electrical engineer, Alan, fine-tuned the result. Bill, meanwhile, created his own Morgan-inspired modification to the exhaust system, "to assist with the breathing", he said; and Tom finished it all off with another of his dedicated paint jobs.

By the time they had finished, I concluded that the tables had finally turned: where I might have needed my head read for instigating the project, Tom, Bill and Alan should be lead away to the proverbial 'funny farm'.

Still, the combination of increased size, higher compression and better airflow added all of fifty-plus horses, to say nothing of the extra acceleration-inducing torque. All this was greeted with keenness as much by Algi, the Morgan-racing banker, as by the rally-driving headlamp-finder who had first criticised the power. Also, for some reason, not only did the new set-up meet the same emission standards as before but, provided the foot was not held flat-to-the-floor, was no less economical.

Of greater interest to the team, though, was the reaction of a German passenger while travelling on an autobahn when two of us were attending an exhibition in Frankfurt. His broad grin, nodding head and transfixed stare, accompanied by, in a barely audible monotone, "fasser, fasser", denoted obvious joy as the Roadster accelerated towards its yet unknown zenith.

What took us all completely by surprise, though, on this first true test of speed, was the discovery that Gavin's difficult-to-make forward ends of the front wings had a most unexpected effect. As the Roadster passed through the magic 'ton' and the needle moved steadily up the dial, the nose, contrary to all expectations for such a style of car, stayed firmly *down*. Somehow, by chance, and chance alone, we had designed enough of a forward wedge on those artistic plans for the result to be aerodynamic as well. Here, again, was yet another bit of luck in the charmed life of a 'car that should never have been'.

As if that was not enough, on returning from Germany, the Roadster was invited to take pride of place at the entrance to the London Classic Motor Show, in that utopian building of old, Alexandra Palace. Ensconced in pole position in the centre of the imposing glass-domed Palm Court, the team turned out in force; as did the spectators and, this time, no negatives were heard to pass the sceptical Londoners' lips.

No sooner was this over, than the much-enlivened machine was back at Goodwood. The revamped circuit, returned as near as possible to the glory days, now had under-cover pits and all around track protection.

With its fitted fan shroud, additional anti-roll bar and increased power, and driven once more by our tutor of old, now chief test driver, the Roadster reached new heights. While accelerating towards a corner as though somehow it would straighten at our approach, I remember simply closing my eyes and praying for deliverance. While drifting through the corner, I was brought up with a jolt at his observation of: "She handles like the current Bentley Brooklands... and that's quite a compliment."

After everything we had all been through, such a statement was more like: "and that's quite astounding!" The 1996 Bentley Brooklands was, as everyone knew, a highly respected super luxury, very expensive semi-sporting motorcar.

Apart from leaving the team in a semi-state of shock, this led to a further invitation: to the holy of holies, to MIRA, Britain's independent vehicle evaluation and test centre.

Situated to the north of Birmingham on a disused wartime airfield, MIRA, with its suitably bannered entrance, is a sprawling mass of corporate buildings, giant evaluation sheds and an array of control towers. Surrounding and intermingled with all this are a range of test tracks and test areas all linked with traffic lights or warning signs via a network of roads and alleyways. Activity is feverish and non-stop with a wide assortment of cars, some recognisable and others in disguise. The combination of exhaust notes mixed with the hum of other machinery produces a constant, but not unpleasant, mechanical drone.

We were soon to discover, however, an altogether different breed of professional to those at Goodwood. There was no 'joie de vivre'; these professionals had but one single-minded mission: to make cars safer and more predictable, not more interesting or more fun, or even necessarily more pleasing to the eye. Moreover, they were neither looking to be loved nor to be thanked and had no intention of confirming the so-judged positive characteristics of their so-stated "home-made vehicle produced by a bunch of amateurs" – or at least certainly not before carrying out some very thorough tests.

"Your suspension needs checking," was their first assessment.

To have made any vehicle travel up, or down, thirty-plus degree slopes, negotiating thirty-odd degree cambers, and over the most unbelievable potholes and humps, was more than enough for such findings to be of no surprise to the amateurs.

Their reply to our observation of, "We don't intend driving on surfaces remotely like these" was "There are plenty of potholes in the back streets of Detroit, you know."

We had no reply to such reasoning, any more than we had to their next assessment: "Just look at this understeer!"

As we travelled in a tight left-hand circle at half throttle, with all four tyres screaming, our inquisitor gently swung the steering wheel from side to side to demonstrate how the front-end appeared altogether unattached. Suddenly, without warning and with the steering at half lock, he took his foot off the throttle. The front tyres dug in with such force that I, as the passenger, was momentarily glued to the door.

"Most cars," he quipped, with just a hint of a smile, "would have flipped toe to tail when doing that,"

"Oh, so that's good is it then?" I said with a note of optimism.

"Well," he began, stony face returning, "not really. You see, for safety reasons, it shouldn't understeer at neutral throttle. Someone might get confused."

Then, in a lighter vein once more: "Now, it's not bad at *this* manoeuvre." As we left the proving circle and began to accelerate down the middle of a four-lane track, I innocently asked: "What's that?"

"I'm going to change lanes," he said casually.

As a precaution, I instinctively grabbed the panic handle. Then, with hands horizontally opposed on the wheel, and with no further warning, he simply crossed arms. No sooner than done, than he uncrossed them again. We literally jumped lanes, like a hare or a rabbit would jump lanes. I have never experienced such a manoeuvre and would certainly not attempt one myself. How the driver and I were not thrown through the window, or from passenger to driver's seat, was a gravity-defying marvel.

To finish, we headed for the high-speed banked circuit to see whether, just possibly, we could fly. On our third time round, while working steadily to the outer edge of the banking, we approached one of the long sweeping banked corners at close to 125 miles per hour. I must have indicated some concern as, with barely eighteen inches separating us from the outside railing, the pilot quipped: "And over we go!" My mind was thrown back to tests on country lanes and around deserted farmyards. Again, I could only sit, pray, hang onto the panic handle, and hope we returned in one piece. Thankfully, we did.

For all that, try as those super-professionals did, for all their tests and re-tests, they were quite incapable of making anything fall off our 'homemade' car. In the end, they had to admit that, although the ride was stiffer and there was some fine-tuning needed to the suspension, the handling was superior to the original Seville. In fact, off the record, one of them confessed that the whole car was rather better than they cared to admit.

They also, as others had before, commented on the surprising quietness at speed. Again, just as Des had suggested, they would have been interested in seeing the result of a wind-tunnel test. They believed, just possibly, that the contortions of Gavin's outer body, when reaching a certain speed, created some sort of freer-flowing envelope, thereby reducing the wind noise.

Those super-professionals also made one other very useful observation, something that would further improve both acceleration and top speed without necessarily worsening the fuel consumption: the final-drive ratio was needlessly high-geared, especially for a truly sporting machine, and should therefore be changed.

Jack, when asked what he thought about such a modification, as always, feet firmly on the ground, merely replied: "That's over to you, mate!"

Bill and Tom had a more positive attitude and, accordingly, Ohio Bob and his parts department in Cleveland were contacted for a new, not inexpensive, set of gears for the differential. While doing so, knowing, despite the belated acclaim and more buoyant classic car market, that there was no possibility of producing more Roadsters, I began to think perhaps I too should be joining the funny farm.

What about the ebullient, ever-optimistic Sandy's reaction to all this? Sadly, of all those involved Sandy was the only one whose company had succumbed to the worst of the early-ninety's recession and we had lost touch with him. If only he could have seen his faith in so obscure a project rewarded to such heights, he would have bubbled and bubbled away to his heart's content.

When the new differential was properly and enjoyably installed and tested, I began to check some of the detail of what I had so far written for the book. I had already gleaned much from members of the team to add to my own experiences. Then, coming to the reference to Robert Faulconer and my Great-uncle Percy, I felt unable, somewhat cheekily, to refer to Robert Faulconer as possibly being the ever-understanding Back-up's "tenth or twentieth cousin, five- or ten-times removed".

In the book Jack had given me at the start, Robert Faulconer, timber tycoon, had joined up with Henry Leland, the man who later became one of the great motor engineers of his time. Together, in the early 1890s, they had set up Leland & Faulconer, the manufacturing company where the first three prototypes and most of the engines and many other components were made prior to the company amalgamating with the Cadillac Automobile Company. This, in turn, was taken over some years later by the budding General Motors Corporation, where it remains as GM's top division in America to this day.

While much is known about Henry Leland, and even the whereabouts of his present-day family, Robert Faulconer, other than being a Detroit industrialist and timber tycoon, was rather less known. On the off chance, as the only possible source of information, I contacted my father-in-law.

"Do you remember several years back I mentioned the coincidence of Robert Faulconer in Detroit spelling his name the same as yours? Well, I'm sure you said that you thought one or more of your relatives had emigrated to the US. Have you any idea about them?"

"No," he replied. "But I know someone who does."

"Oh, who?" I asked.

"It was funny really. Some time back, I was in a queue at the bank and the man in front of me had a camera slung over his shoulder with 'Revd Jim Faulconer' stencilled on it, with 'Faulconer' spelt our same way." He paused, then went on: "Well, I didn't feel I could leave it at that, so I tapped him on the shoulder and said, 'Hello, we must be related.'"

"What did he say?" I asked, more than a little surprised at my father-in-law's break with his normal tradition of total silence with strangers in public.

"Well, we got to talking. He was American and not only was he a man of the cloth, he also turned out to be a genealogist and had written a book about the Faulconers of America."

"How incredible," I interjected. "What a coincidence. Have you kept in touch? Can we write and ask him about Robert Faulconer?"

"I can do better than that. After returning to America, he sent me a copy of his book. You can borrow it and look up the detail for yourself."

On receiving the book, I set about searching for Robert of Detroit, around 1875 to 1900. I came across several Roberts, along with their relationships to each other, but none fitted. How ridiculous, I thought, the genealogist has missed him out.

"Your friend's overlooked the 'motoring' Faulconer," I said to my father-in-law when next we spoke, finishing off with, as any true motoring devotee would: "He's missed the most important of them all!"

"Well, send me a copy of the detail in the book and I'll send it off to him with a letter."

Several months passed with no reply. Perhaps we had stumped, possibly even embarrassed, the Reverend Jim. Then, eventually, came the response explaining how, after receiving the letter, he had been unable to find any substantial information on Robert Faulconer, other than the references to him regarding Leland & Faulconer. The Reverend Jim went on to explain how, when time had allowed, he had gone to the "great genealogical library" in Fort Wayne, Indiana. There, in the 1900 Detroit census, he had found Robert, along with his wife Elizabeth and three daughters, Lillian, Margaret and Kathleen. To his surprise, and now to ours too, recorded against Robert's name was "born in England".

The Reverend Jim finished by thanking us for bringing this "prosperous clan-member" to his attention and to point out that, as Robert's wife was recorded as "born in Michigan", Robert had presumably come to the United States as a single young man sometime just after the Civil War. We should therefore attempt to trace him at our end. The ball was firmly back in our court.

On seeing the names of Robert's daughters, my father-in-law swallowed hard and scratched his head. There was something familiar about two of the names, Margaret and Kathleen. He had long ago known of cousins in America with those same Christian names, and they would have been born around that time. Yet, to the best of his knowledge, they were not Faulconer relations, but some other offshoot from another part of his family.

If he or we, several years earlier, had bothered to check in amongst old family papers, we would have discovered that Great-great-uncle Robert Charles Faulconer, had, in his early twenties sometime around 1870, emigrated to America. When there, or so it would appear from a letter written by him around 1900, he had fallen in love with both lady and land. He managed to capture the heart of Elizabeth Emmons, the daughter of Judge H H Emmons of Detroit, and, having become an American citizen, remained there until his death at the age of 61, in 1907. Although the family eventually moved away from Detroit, he, his wife and several daughters are buried alongside the Emmons family in Elmwood Cemetery, Detroit.

So the prominent Detroit businessman who had helped found a well-known make of motorcar turned out to be the brother of 'Uncle Ruddy' who, in strict contrast, was an arch coaching revivalist in England, and therefore cared little for the twentieth century's new-fangled transport. No doubt this love of horse and reins, many photographs of which still survive, along with Robert having had no sons to carry on the Faulconer name, was why the family had over-looked Robert's input to the American dream.

Not only did we uncover this unexpected family link of nearly a century earlier, we also succeeded in tracking down Robert's great-grandson. Such a discovery, and the family reunion that followed, almost on its own, counted for a thousand hours in that dank underlit barn. As one elderly English relative wryly observed: "If only we had known, we could all have driven around in huge, comfortable, glamorous American cars – what sport!"

Therefore, as improbable and as extraordinary as it may seem, the great great uncle on one side had, after all, provided help in making the long-since-deceased great uncle's very first car on the other. Such a link was eerie to say the least and was certainly a twist that nobody could have foreseen – not even the indomitable Des.

When told, Des went silent for the only time I can recall. Conversely, Frank, with his relaxed countryman's view, merely said: "Wouldn't you rather have known about it before you became involved in building the Roadster?"

After some thought, I replied: "Well, everything would have got off to the wrong start. Just imagine the arguments: 'Uncle Robert wouldn't have liked this', or 'Uncle Robert wouldn't have done that'... it would have been never-ending. No, I think not."

"I take your point," Frank observed with a smile, "Yes, and you would have said: 'But Uncle Percy was the customer and he would have wanted this or that'. Yes, you're right, it could have been tricky!"

Gavin, as always, had a novel approach: "So, you should have been driven to the church in a *foreign* car when you were married, not some English machine as you once told me." At which, with one of his cheeky chuckles, he threw back at me the observation I had made about his family when first we met: "See, it was 'in the blood' all along!"

Bill was more pragmatic. "What does that make you?" he ventured, as though the newfound link with a world-renowned motor manufacturer's past should have some elevated bearing on the 'link's' husband, especially with my long preoccupation with the marque.

"The mechanic and the chauffeur!" was my immediate response, as I thought of the Back-up's ultimate turning of the tables.

Bill's wry smile was followed by a more relevant question: "Has she driven the Roadster yet?"

"Yes," came the answer, then after a short sucking of teeth, "but not unaccompanied!"

Bill had to laugh. So did Paul, our irascible trimmer, when I suggested that maybe the timber tycoon had been the cause of Detroit having "run out of trees", Paul well remembering his remark about "meltable wood".

Back in the present, as we faced the realisation that old Sevilles were getting older and to upgrade the Roadster's technology would mean re-drawing the plans, a group of us decided to club together and rescue the redundant prototype from its non-motoring corporate owner. Having done so, we felt we could hardly let the infamous one-off sink into semi-obscurity. There had to be some interesting occupation for such a machine.

The answer was not long in coming. Just as years earlier on super-hot days heading up those long African hills, steam emerging from the bonnet, the old family Ford had "evaporated", or so they said, so caution was about to evaporate to the winds of a different kind. With a burst of renewed passion, several of us declared: "Why not fly the flag for team, town, corporation – and family too for that matter – and do a bit of racing after all?"

And with that, a story that had begun as the tale of a so-styled "good investment", headed deeper into new and altogether unknown territory.

14. Dangerous Ploy

"Why not enter the Pomeroy?" suggested our old rallying friend – that finder of headlamps and lover of six-hundred horses – when asked what he thought about having a go on the track.

"What's that?" I asked, more than mildly concerned at the sound of something so grand.

"Oh, it's nothing too strenuous old boy... it's a sort of endurance trial. You know, a few tests and a bit of a joint sprint. It's great fun and all sorts of cars enter. The Vintage Sports-Car Club organise it at Silverstone in February each year. You have to be a member, though... but I'll sort that out."

"Thank you," I said, my early misgivings escalating at the mention of the nation's premier motor-racing circuit.

"Good idea," replied Algi, a glint in his eye at having been first with such an idea when he suggested we took to the track several years earlier. "Yes, the Pomeroy's always great fun. A Seville in the Pomeroy... that should raise a few eyebrows." Then, seeing my concern, added: "Don't worry, we'll see you through everything."

Membership of the Vintage Sports-Car Club was arranged and the competition entered. No sooner done, than I was informed that, by long-standing tradition, cars were always driven by their owners or, in our case, their keepers. Furthermore, a full race licence was needed, driving test and all.

I was neither happy nor amused at the trap into which I had fallen. The lover of six hundred horses and Algi, the Morgan-racing banker, would, I hoped, live up to their assurances and properly back me up.

"Oh come now, the licence is just a formality," was Algi's next reassuring ploy, "Don't be such a worrier. It'll be no trouble at all. Of course we'll get you through."

Would they just? They were nowhere to be seen when, a week before the event, I found myself about to sit a stiff written exam, followed by an even stiffer driving test in a car with manual gears and a steering wheel on the right. The majority of American cars, for some fifty years or more, have not had manual gears and only recently, after a similar length of time, are some again offering the option of right-hand drive.

In desperation, I contacted Frank. Although he had long since ended his racing career, which he had interspersed with his seasonal farming activities, tradition still ran strong: Frank's son now raced. Somehow, with their help, I passed. Then, the day before the event, having captured Algi, just as I had captured him the night before his visit to the barn several years earlier: disaster. He somehow caused a thermometer to indicate 102 degrees and remained firmly bed-ridden.

My other advisor proved to be little better. When telephoned for advice on steering technique, I received a simple monologue ending with: "Oh, don't worry, old boy, that's just detail. No, really, don't worry... I once drove past the stands at 140 miles an hour with both hands in the air!"

Memories of Gavin's so-called completed bodywork flashed to mind: "Don't worry... I'll come and sort it out at the weekend." That "don't worry" had taken a full two months to put right. What was I supposed to do now: arrive at Silverstone to announce: "Here I am, which end of the car would you like me to stick the number on?" or even, "Which way round does the track go?"

Once more, Frank was my only hope. I telephoned him. At first, there was no reply. Then his wife answered. She must have detected the note of near panic in my voice; and Frank was summoned forthwith, whether from inside a turkey coup or loyally tending one of his cherished classic cars was irrelevant. I explained my predicament, terror now rising to a crescendo. Thankfully, message received, he agreed to join me early next morning.

We met up at six and set off in patchy winter fog. We arrived in the half-light to find all sorts of cars as predicted. What my helpers had never dared explain was that these would consist of historic racing icons ranging from the beginning of the last century, through the wildcats of the thirties – including some amazing Bentley with an aero-engine – to the super-classics of the sixties and seventies. There were Aston Martins, Ferraris, Jaguars and all, and even some of the latest turbo-charged technology from the eighties and nineties.

Having signed on, I was ushered to a holding area to wait my turn for the first event. Despite a heavy clouded sky, the track was dry and a friendly atmosphere prevailed. The early trials went well enough, even receiving praise for my prowess on the slalom: adequately zigzagging from point-to-point, then sprinting ably down the track. I was not too popular, though, during the braking test when, having pulled up quicker than expected, I briefly lifted my foot, only to jam it down again and finish half-sideways between two stony-faced officials. Even after a polite, apologetic smile, they moved not a muscle and uttered not a word.

When the listings for the sprints were posted on the notice board, as best as Frank could determine, I would be starting as tail-ender in the fastest of the three trials. Despite my obvious concern at being with the Astons, Jaguars, turbo-Porches and the like, the tail-end position well suited Algi's advice: "Just follow the others and get a feel of things... you'll soon get the hang of it."

Unfortunately Frank had misread the list. Due partly to the dubious honour of the Roadster having been given the event's highest-ever handicap – calculated by some long-standing unfathomable formula – and partly to keeper and machine having done well enough in the morning trials, we had been placed at the front – in pole position – alongside one of the Porsches: and on a now very wet track.

Before I could fully grasp the situation, or fathom whether this was some great honour, or the race committee had taken complete leave of their senses, the pace car was moving off and the race about to start. Two circuits later, with the start flag waved by yet another sober-faced marshal, we were off.

Ever conscious from within an ultra-soundproofed cab of the

muted roar of engines round about, I partly did what I had been told: "Put your foot hard to the floor along the main straight and keep accelerating past the stands. That's a must," they had said. I did not, I am pleased to say, let go of the steering wheel. As the corner loomed, time to slow and change down; foot not-too-hard on the brake, then into the second of those three, seemingly indestructible, automatic gears. Four-and-a-bit thousand pounds began to slow, the gear engaged with an imperceptible jerk. Too wet, too late, tarmac and tyres parted at the rear.

An instinctive 'turn into the skid' – as long-since taught on mud roads in Africa – and the front parted company too. As the tail began to move to the left, I found myself in a world within a world, a silent world inside the cab, quite detached from the one outside. A gently clockwise-rotating vista that, as best my mind could absorb, was still moving at a terrifying, almost incomprehensible speed along the track.

First to pass across my revolving view is the Porsche, side on; the driver's face cast in stone, intense and concentrating. Then, approaching from the right, grilles and headlights advancing towards a very vulnerable, highly polished side, comes a C-type Jaguar, or is it the D-type, and something else alongside. An eternity of a milli-second later and they are approaching head on – we must collide. Then, as if by some psychic awakening, I realise that my silent separate world is still travelling at the same speed as them: but in reverse.

As we continue on the three-quarter circle, still hurtling down the track, the throng of supercars – now coming from my left – edges closer all the time. We begin to slow; the corner is on us. What will be the damage and what will be the aftermath for which I will have to answer?

Suddenly, still broadside across the field, the tyres begin to grip. Fear, of a type as seldom known, came with a mighty rush. With a flick of the wheel – by instinct or providence or a combination of both – and, just in time, we are off that track. There, stunned and motionless, I sit while the mighty horde shoot by.

When, at length, the final taillight had disappeared from view and a deep breath had been inhaled and released, then and only then did I rejoin that other world. Never was I so happy to step out, and almost up, into the loose gravel and walk away in one piece: and, miraculously, from a completely undamaged car.

Unceremoniously, some more stony-faced officials removed the Roadster from its gravelly den – just like the Ford from the ford in Africa – at which there was only one question I could ask: "*Who* was I supposed to follow?"

"Why didn't you let someone overtake you?" came the innocent suggestion from she who had once tried to make an Aston fly.

Such a suggestion was unanswerable. Whether a joint sprint, a trial or an out-and-out race, the thought of letting anyone overtake never crossed my mind, any more than it would have crossed Algi's mind or that of headlamp-finding, self-acclaimed "hands in the air".

I continued to joke as best I could, and gave as good a showing to all around of being relaxed. In truth, bubbling up from within was the realisation that the Roadster and I should never have entered this "lots of fun" with "all sorts of cars". A gentle flag-waving had ended up in a flag burying. Des was right: we should have been "put away", as he had said, for contemplating such a thing.

As Frank and I made our way home, we discussed what next to do. Should I, or we, attempt to regain a semblance of credibility for the Roadster or should we just walk away and pretend nothing had happened? Any rational thoughts were hardly helped by the constant drone of Bill's better-breathing exhaust, jammed firmly open with pebbles from our backward slide.

"There are two things," Frank shouted over the din. "First, you must fit the right tyres. Hardwearing American tyres are not suitable for racing in wet weather, any more than old-type Michelin's were. In America, they tend to race on banked circuits and generally cancel if it rains."

"I'm sure you're right," I said, nodding hard, while barely being heard. "And what's the other?" I yelled over the racket.

"If you intend to regain full credibility... both of you and the car... you need a whole lot more practice."

He was right on that, for sure: in one short experience, I had discovered that encounters with African mud, Middle East sand dunes and German autobahns was no substitute for practice on a racetrack. Whether I had, or I had not, passed my sell-by date for this sport, the Roadster had to have a better racing conclusion – and I suppose, in all honesty, so should I. At that, we gave up competing with Bill's better-breathing and continued home.

The following week, Bill and I headed off to Tom to check for underside damage and remove what Tom unkindly referred to as the "kitty litter" from the exhaust system – not to mention every other under-chassis nook and cranny. As Tom chattered away, sometimes to us and sometimes to himself, while steadily picking out the pebbles, Bill made one of his chin-rubbing suggestions: "What about sprints and hill climbs,"

"What about them?" I asked.

"Well, why not join a sprint or hill-climb club?" he suggested, "and involve the Roadster in some of those events."

Bill duly gave me some contacts and, after talking the idea over with Frank, I took the plunge.

"Yes," said the competition secretary of the Sevenoaks & District Motor Club on the telephone, "and what's the car?"

"It's a modified Seville," I said without hesitation and then, to avoid any adverse comment, quickly added: "We've had it in the Pomeroy… it did quite well in the quarter mile and the slalom, but we didn't quite finish the trial… I was one of several who came off in the wet."

There was a moment's silence, no doubt while he fully digested the combination of American car and the involuntary exiting of a premier racetrack. At that point, no Cadillac had raced since the early fifties when two of them, one nicknamed 'Le Monstre', entered Le Mans. Although they had both done surprisingly well, I refrained from using this fact as a door opener. I very much doubted my potential ally would have heard of this long-forgotten invasion from across the Atlantic.

"That's unusual," came the eventual response, followed by, "Isn't it a bit big for racing?"

"Not really, the Seville was considered a sort-of 'compact' by the Americans." I answered, trying to sound reasonably intelligent and believable.

"Oh, I see… well, I'll send you a list of events. Try to make the one at Crystal Palace. That's open to the general public as spectators, and they always like anything unusual."

"Thanks," I said, and hung up before potentially upsetting a fine balance between fact and fiction. He must have been very trusting, I thought: yet again, car and driver seemed to have been accepted on

162

face value.

I attended the first event accompanied by family only: no outside watchers please, especially experienced ones. All went as well as could be expected. The fact that I remained firmly on the start line while the green light was run through three times and missed the corner for the second lap, not once but twice, were, with great generosity, put down to being a beginner. On the other hand, that I should arrive without a timing strut was seen by the official scrutineer as flippancy, especially when I inferred that I had no idea to what he was referring.

"Why do you imagine all the other entrants have those black uprights bolted on the front of their cars. Do you think they're there for decoration?"

I had, in fact, thought they were some symbol of the racing fraternity to which I had not yet aspired. Still, having discovered that the scrutineer held similar sway over all who came under his authority as Adolf held over those who required an annual MoT, I declined to answer. When he explained, at great length, that these frontal additions were for cutting the beam of the timing-light to within a hundredth of a second, I offered an apology. Eventually, he forced a smile, stuck a "passed" on the windscreen and sent me on my way.

Successive events, often with Bill or Frank accompanying, became more relaxed and, generally, more successful. After each, we returned the car to Tom to cast his eagle mechanical eye over anything that might have succumbed to the added stress. Occasionally, also, I went off to see Jack to check the forward structure that took the brunt of the heavy cornering.

Thus, some much-needed practice and some general overall testing was gained before confronting a mass of Londoners in Crystal Palace Park; any number of whom might jeer rather than cheer at the antics of some apparent playboy in his large and seemingly expensive toy.

When the time came, all manner of machines, to say nothing of all manner of spectators, came to enjoy the warm and sunny early summer's day in that pleasant all-green setting in South London. Although the glass palace itself had long since gone, destroyed by fire in the nineteen-thirties, the park, with its pleasant undulating close-cropped lawns and dotted trees, had been the venue until twenty years earlier of London's only race circuit. Part of the original racetrack, winding through the gentle slopes in amongst the trees, remained and, on this, we would each now pit our skills.

"You got the air-conditioning on, young man?" came drifting through the window as I sat in the queue waiting for the first run. "Yes," I replied; to which the onlooker wandered off shaking his head, either in disbelief that there should be air-conditioning in such a car, or that anybody should think of using it when racing. True, with the 'compressor' being a potential power reducer and the 'evaporator' in front of the radiator capable of causing another heat-test failure, once on the track, the air-conditioning was firmly switched to off.

"Gosh! Which car are you driving?" came a semi-awed retort as I wandered checking the course before the next run.

"The two-tone blue one," I answered, smiling blankly and pointing across the track; then backing away, fearful that some other question would be one to which I had no answer. Looking down at my driver's overalls – compulsory for all who drove – I understood how the smiling couple standing opposite had guessed. Little, though, were they to realise how misguided was their admiration.

"Turn on the Nitro, mate," resounded from the crowd, as I sat on the grid waiting for the start light to change from red to green on the second run. Prompted no doubt by the unexplained roar at the start of the previous run, the remark received instant compliance. With a flick of the switch, Bill's better breathing enticed a further cheer in return.

"Here comes Cruella DeVille," someone was heard to say, as the dark blue sleek machine headed towards them along the straight; "There go David and Goliath!" someone else noted, as a miniature Austin Seven racer pulled up alongside the two-ton racing Seville.

In the end, the day proved most enjoyable, and those who came to support the steadily improving racing duo seemed to enjoy it too. As the months passed, car and driver became more as one, and always stayed firmly on the track. Then, as the season drew to a close, and after Tom had given the Roadster an ongoing all clear, the day came for the real test of the 'moderately elderly man' and the 'moderately young machine'. The Jaguar invitation day, to be held in an elegant country park in the mid-west, was the Jaguar Club's annual highlight.

With an eight o'clock start, we booked into a pub nearby to make the early morning start.

Cars and competitors arrived in the early autumn mist, entering the park through stately wrought-iron gates. The drive ahead, stretching up into the middle distance and flanked by undulating lawns and mature trees, their lower branches neatly clipped by domestic animals and wildlife alike, was brought to a close by a superb colonnaded magnificence from a former age. Such splendour had a hugely spirit-lifting effect: like royalty "out for a day of play".

Discovering that the competitors in our class were not normal Jaguar saloons, as we had naively assumed, but highly tuned machines, some with internal stiffeners, and all stripped of carpets, seats and every other excess weight, we descended back to earth with a jolt. Added to that, as we approached to introduce ourselves, their drivers were discussing milli-second timings at events from all around the country, and from abroad too.

We smiled politely, answered questions, and explained away our presence as best we could. The signing on and the fixing of the timing strut were simple enough procedures now. The positioning of numbers, stripping-off of hubcaps and the removal of the spare wheel were also straightforward, scrutineering by now having become a mere formality.

There for encouragement were the ever-supportive farmer Frank, cigarette-rolling Bill and a member of the Roadster's new syndicate with his entire family, in-laws and all. We sat waiting for the timed runs to begin, more than a little apprehensive. Eventually, on the first run, much to the surprise of all, we were far from last. There followed accu-sations that so large an engine was excessive and out of keeping with such an event. To this, we pointed out that their Jaguars were a good thousand pounds lighter than was our modified Seville, and with engines and power-trains more in tune with the occasion – and not that small either.

On the next run, to the extreme consternation of one of the more competitive drivers, we were a mere two hundredth's of a second behind him. Returning to our holding position, their attitude had begun to change.

"Could I sit inside … just for a second?" one of them asked.

"Yes," I replied, not wanting to hold against them for earlier disagreements.

"Very comfortable, yes, very comfortable," he repeated, while swinging on the steering and humming to himself. Then another asked if he could try too.

Pleased no longer to be treated as some oddity from some other world, Bill began to delight in their budding zeal. That these hardened racers, so many of whom he had come across over the years, should feel there was, after all, some merit to a soundproof, air-conditioned racer was an added reward for all those underpaid hours in Frank's underlit, often near freezing barn. That they should also view with certain affection the electric armchair seats, each weighing nearly a hundred pounds, was even more reward.

"What's this for?" asked one, pointing to a switch on the dashboard.

"Well," I chipped in, not wanting the intricacies of Alan's electronic fuel enricher combined with Bill's own electro-mechanical better-breathing exhaust divulged to one and all, "let's just say it adds a bit of power at higher revs,"

"The switch next to it, though," I added, being a bit more forth-coming, "is for the town and country horns. The old-time horns out front are fairly useless at speed, and the seventies pair under the bonnet are, for want of a better description, somewhat impolite when driving around at shows."

As each of the Jaguar drivers, one after the other, clambered in and, when everything had been demonstrated to their satisfaction, out again, I began to wonder what Algi and hands-in-the-air had led us into. A mere two hundredths of a second behind one of these highly prepared machines, was closer than any of us could have dared.

Should I or should I not, I thought, as we left to prepare for the final run, put in my all and attempt to beat the unbeatable? Without any reference to Bill or Frank, I contemplated long and hard, taking account of risk to older man and newer machine. In the end, there was only one answer: may the best man – and machine – win.

While waiting on the start with the light at red, having – as I had recently been taught – spun the tyres on the tar to improve their grip, I tried to relax. The light turned green. With barely a spin, and exhaust roaring, we were off up his lordship's drive in the fifty-plus-mile-an-hour bottom gear. When the engine reached full pitch, up to second.

As the trees flashed past and the end of the straight came ever closer, into top and still accelerating. Then, as our aristocratic host's front door neared and the tight right-hand bend came closer into view – mere hay bales to fend off any speeding Anglo-American mass – I eyed the markers up ahead: the three-hundred-yard, the two-hundred-yard and the one-hundred-yard.

With foot remaining to the floor past the three-hundred, foot still hard down at the two-hundred – when normal everyday driving would have both feet on the brake – my brain by now was barely aware of the danger fast approaching. Now: it had to be. I dared not wait a moment longer: foot firmly on those four-wheel power disc brakes, but not so hard as to produce a skid. Yes, just in time; and they prove straight and true as well.

Off with the brake and fling the wheel to the right. The nose should bite, bite it does and round we go, missing bales and kerbs by only inches. Down to bottom again and foot to the floor once more. Next corner; brake again, this time easing the tail on the throttle around a sweeping left. Foot flat again as we turn gently to the right, then up to second as we head into the park and towards the woods, accelerating hard all the way.

Down the hill we charge and back into top. Up the other side, sweeping to the right; over the rise, suspension lifting, and down on the other side, suspension firming again. Then, as trees flash past, we hurtle, at I know not what speed, towards the marshals at the end. I shoot past, foot still to the floor. Then, and only then, did I lift off. I braked and slowed and braked some more, then, drawing almost to a halt, turned and headed onto the grass to park and await the challengers. For sure, I could have done no better.

Each, in turn, came into view, braked, slowed and parked alongside, composed and unspeaking. Then my direct rival appeared, engine roaring, also only braking when well past the line. He turned, slowed to a crawl and parked beside. He stumbled out, exhaustion written across his face.

"Not even a milli-second," he exclaimed, "could I have shaved off that run. Even with another five runs, I could have done no better."

He looked towards me for some hint of how I felt I might have fared. I never doubted I must have shaved a little off my time; but could our smooth-riding Roadster really have beaten him? Only the official times would tell. When they did, they told the story well enough. I had indeed improved my time. Yet, for all his worries, my rival had bettered his by just a fraction more. He had won the day, as I was always sure he must.

We smiled across the expanse that separated our opposing teams. There was nothing to say. The Roadster was never intended to be a racing car, and to have performed the way it had was remarkable to say the very least. The team itself, and everyone involved in the construction, had every right to be proud. So too, should the original designers and engineers, who created that luxury, silent, gliding late-seventies Seville, have just as much right.

Bill was ecstatic. "What about…?" he started as we walked away.

Frank and I saw the glint in his eye, and stopped him in his tracks. "I think we had best leave well alone," I said.

"Yes," Frank added, "I hardly think you should start throwing out the air-conditioning, the electric armchair seats, or anything else for that matter, to gain some extra seconds. Anyway, Des would have a fit… he'd most probably shoot the lot of us on sight!"

Bill laughed, as did we all. The flag had been flown, and very convincingly too, and car and driver were at last forgiven for their erratic racing start, just as the driver now forgave those who had lead him down such a path. There was no need of any additional idiotic risks in pursuit of further aims. To start making modifications to the modifications after what we had been through would only prove that we really should perhaps be *committed* after all.

That said, little did any of us realise as we headed home that, with its added acclaim, our exotic one-off semi-retired racing Roadster was about to be embroiled in something more.

15. Further Links

As the dust settled on a short but eventful racing career and as autumn gave way to the last months of the Millennium, I found myself increasingly involved with various motor clubs. In particular were the Cadillac LaSalle Club of America, which I had joined on hearing of its existence through the television show 'Coltraine and a Cadillac', and the Cadillac Owners Club of Great Britain, on seeing their name in a magazine.

When the British club heard of the Faulconer connection – and on their eventual acceptance of a now fully-acclaimed modified Seville – I was given the grand title of Club's Liaison Officer and instructed to foster Trans-Atlantic links. Then, when the magazine editor unexpectedly stepped down, there being no volunteer to succeed him, I was volunteered for that as well.

Whenever in America after that, whether on company business or on holiday, I was instructed to take photos for the club magazine or even find some spare part or other; and I was always to be sure to arrange my itinerary around the US club's 'Grand National', their annual get-together. Attending one of these, not long after the Roadster had been written up in a couple of US publications expounding, amongst other things, its prowess on the racetrack, I was approached with an altogether different request.

"Why don't you," queried the representative from Virginia, "organise an international show in England? With your racing activities and all, you must know plenty of people who would get involved."

"Yes, Mr. Englishman," joined in the Texas counterpart, "why not do just that and we'll all come and visit you." Then, with a broad Texas grin, continuing with: "I'll bring my best car... cow-horns and all... and even have a race with that *desecrated* Seville of yours!"

"OK, what about 2003, the year after your centenary celebrations in Detroit," then assuming the "desecrated" to be in jest, added, "but you can leave out the racing bit... *I & it* have retired!"

"Done," they both replied, and within the hour the two southerners had informed the American club's international representative, who lived in the north, that a major club meet was irrevocably fixed in

England for 2003.

How, I thought, had I been so easily cornered, and without even the ability to consult the British club? Still, previous trips to the American annual event had had their moments, and I really should have been prepared. At my first Grand National in Albany, upper New York state, several years earlier, I had fallen straight into a trap set by none other than the American club's illustrious co-founder from way back in 1958, 'Norm', as he was affectionately known.

Norm, earlier that year, had written an article in the American club magazine referring to the confusion often felt over the early days of the newly established marque and the latter days of Leland & Faulconer Manufacturing. Having just discovered the Faulconer link, and not realising Norm's elevated position in the club, I had somewhat impertinently telephoned him to say that my father-in-law had discovered the answer in amongst his family papers. As I continued my ramblings, Norm's patience proved boundless. Instead of abruptly ending the conversation, as surely he should have, we had continued to talk on at length.

Several months after that at the Albany event, firmly on his own home ground, he and I and one neé Faulconer were about to meet for the first time:

"Raarbet," he had said in his mid-west semi-drawl, as we all arrived almost at exactly the same time in the designated hotel lobby – we having flown in from England, and he and his wife having driven all the way from Arizona – "We meet at last." Then, as he looked to my right, his smile warming: "And this must be 'Miss' Fall-con-er."

"Yes," she replied, as Norm forced himself from his wheelchair, brushing objections aside.

"And you," I interjected, as the hand-shakes started all around, "must be the one and only Norm!"

Barely twenty-four hours after that meeting, in front of some five hundred guests at the meet's grand banquet and without any warning, the toastmaster announced: "Will you all please welcome the return of our co-founder's family. Could Robert Faulconer's great-grand-niece please stand up."

The great-grand-niece, after a friendly kick under the table from me, rose to her feet, smiled and waved.

"Gotcha, Raarbet!" came an outstretched gun-finger across the table from Norm; while moments later from underneath the table I received as good, if not better than I had given earlier.

That was then. Now, several years later, I was being asked to help set up an international club event, a Grand International no less.

On returning to England, I discussed the idea with the UK club. "Agreed", said the chairman; "Definitely", said the show organiser; "Yes, yes," replied the treasurer, inspecting his accounts; and the secretary, deadpanned as always, followed suit by raising a hand.

Such a function, although requiring more work and organisation than at first appeared, would always produce a turnout of a hundred or so quality cars from the fifties, sixties and seventies. However, to be truly international and a bit special, it needed more, something of an unusual or even more British nature.

One item came quickly to mind: a much-hailed connection with an English entrepreneur way back in the early 1900s.

Frederic Stanley Bennett, as recorded in all literature on the marque, had imported the first Cadillac into England in early 1903, the company's very first full production year. As UK agent from then until the First World War, he had driven various models in a variety of hill-climbs and endurance trials, often winning in his class and just as often being written up in the press.

Mr Bennett had also taken it upon himself to challenge the Royal Automobile Club over the interchangability of car parts, culminating, in 1908, in the winning of the coveted RAC Dewar Trophy, awarded for motoring innovation. Then, when the company brought out the first electric self-starter and all-electric lighting in 1913, he managed a second Dewar Trophy win.

After all this time, though, would we be able to locate anything relating to this long-gone bit of history? Brooklands, where the first Dewar Trophy challenge had taken place, was still partly intact and the Royal Automobile Club was as much a prominent landmark in London on the south side of Pall Mall as it always has been. There was one other reference to Mr Bennett that, rightly or wrongly, I had ignored for several years.

My elderly mother, on the discovery of the Faulconer connection, had availed herself of some relevant literature and read up anything and everything. After which, whenever an opportunity arose, she would interrupt the conversation to add her own 'two penneth'.

"I see there was someone called 'Bennett' involved with Cadillac motorcars in the early days in London?" would filter through a relaxed Sunday lunch conversation. "Your grandfather had a friend named Bennett who had something to do with cars in London. 'I'm off to see old Bennett', he would say, and always with a smile. I believe they met at Crewe doing engineering together... he must be one and the same!"

"Yes Mother," I would reply on each occasion, "I'm sure he was," and the matter was always left at that. It was difficult enough to swallow the Faulconer link without adding this apparent family one-upmanship. All the same, as the years passed, she refused to back down. Whenever the Faulconer name was mentioned, the same chirp was sure to be heard: "Yes, and don't forget your grandfather's friend, Mr Bennett."

Now, with the need for some local input to the impending Grand International, was the time to delve further. Spurred on by a growing sense of curiosity about my grandfather and his friends of old, could there, I thought, be any truth in what my sprightly, nearly ninety-year-old mother attested?

The Royal Automobile Club, with its links both to the early endurance trials as well as the Dewar Trophy, seemed as good a starting point. The club had already helped by supplying information on the two Dewar Trophy wins. I contacted them again and asked for anything they had on Mr Bennett.

What I received left me no better off. Frederic Bennett had, by any motoring standards, performed some extraordinary feats in his time, but there seemed little or no personal detail on him. I continued to comb any other references I could lay hands on.

In 'Cadillac The Complete History', by Maurice Hendry, I found two useful clues. There was mention of Frederic Bennett being an engineer – not just the super-salesman as insinuated in other references – and that he was born in 1874.

"In what year was grandfather born?" I asked my mother.

"1874," she replied. "Why?"

"I'm looking into something," I said, "I'll let you know."

So Grandfather and Frederic Bennett were, if nothing else, the same age, and both were engineers. This was becoming a little uncanny. Still, other than my mother's continual insistence on the two being friends, it was still mere chance.

Then I remembered a document Maurice Hendry had sent me from his home in New Zealand after the long telephone discussion we had had about Robert Faulconer. It was a copy of a letter from Veteran & Vintage magazine to Maurice in reply to his attempt, nearly thirty years earlier, to find a member of the Bennett family. According to the letter, Frederic Bennett had kept his original 1903 single-cylinder car, then passed it on to his son. The letter then went on to say that the son, Lt. Cdr. G. F. Bennett, was believed to be living abroad, and therefore the trail had gone cold.

Veteran & Vintage magazine, I discovered, had been linked to Beaulieu and the National Motor Museum. This, therefore, had to be my next port of call. The museum agreed to photocopy and send me all they had on Frederic Bennett. When received, these produced a somewhat broader picture.

The first item that struck me, which seemed most unusual, was a news picture of a bowler-hatted man squeezed into a miniature car driving down Pall Mall. Referred only to as 'Queen Alexandra's Baby Cadillac', the caption explained that this third-scale replica of a 1912 open tourer was propelled by the all-new-at-the-time electric self-starter. The one-of-a-kind had been made under Frederic Bennett's direction in London to promote this revolutionary innovation both in the United Kingdom and mainland Europe. The article went on to explain that Queen Alexandra, King Edward VII's wife, had later bought the car for her grandson, Prince Olaf of Norway.

Although a number of books stated that just one of these cars existed, which had eventually been given to Henry Leland's grandson in America on his fifth birthday, according to yet another article, another of these baby Bennett cars had gone to the then King of Siam. How, I thought, could two such unusual fully-working third-scale electric cars, capable of travelling some 15 miles on one battery charge at speeds of up to 12mph, appear so vaguely recorded in general motoring history? In fact, exactly how many were there; and could there, I wondered, with our event in mind, be any chance that at least one still existed?

First off, I was told to try the Royal Archives at Windsor. I did, to which, amazingly, I was informed that one such little car had been bought from Mr F S Bennett on 28th January 1913 for the princely sum of £62; but there the information stopped. The archivist suggested I approach the Norwegian Royal Household through the Norwegian Embassy in London.

The English switchboard operator at the Embassy chuckled nervously at my request and put me through to someone else. Once connected, I repeated my, by now, semi-monotone spiel, and waited for the inevitable silence.

"Yes," said the softly spoken Norwegian lady, "I think I know the car you mean."

"What?" I enquired, with incredulity. "How could you know of this car when it was last written about in England nearly ninety years ago?"

"That is in England," came the reply, "in Norway, this little car is very well known. It is, I think, the Norwegians' most favourite car. It was placed on loan to the Norsk Teknisk Museum in Oslo many years ago by Prince Olaf, before he became King Olaf." There was a moment's hesitation before she continued: "I will give you the museum's telephone number... you can call them and see for yourself."

The Director of the museum was immediate in his reply: "Yes, certainly, she is here. I have her sitting outside my door. Yes, Prince Olaf's little car has always been one of our most favourite exhibits. In fact, the Crown Prince made a special visit here at the Millennium to

174

inspect her. Maybe she needs a little attention... and it would be nice to have a glass cover to protect her too."

I had to laugh, and he laughed too when I told him how I had tracked the elusive machine, literally, to his doorstep. He explained that over the years a number of people from England had contacted the museum, enquiring about the little car. He offered to send me information: copies of letters sent in by well-wishers from England, photographs taken by the museum and those of its early days with the young princes. One of the letters clearly referring to there having been not one but two cars, the other having gone to the young Wilfred Leland in America. Of that car, last seen in pieces in America sometime in the mid-nineteen-seventies, there seemed no clue to its eventual fate. Still, that part of the mystery was now solved.

What, though, of the third car sold to the King of Siam, the grandson of the much romanticised King Rama IV of 'The King & I' and 'Anna and the King of Siam' fame. We eventually discovered that this one, made some time after the first two, remained with the King's descendents right up until 1990s, after which the Japanese entered the fray and locked it away, we know not where. With the sleuthing over, we asked The Director of the Norsk Teknisk Museum if there was any possibility of his four-wheel charge joining us in England at our forth-coming special event. He would, he said, look into the possibility and let us know, cost being the main problem both for them and for us.

The second item of interest in the papers from Beaulieu was in an article about Frederic Bennett's golden jubilee re-run of the 1903 RAC Reliability Trial. That really got me, and properly spiked my disbelieving guns. Towards the middle, the article unequivocally stated that Frederic Stanley Bennett "took an engineering degree at Owens College, Manchester, and began his working life as an engineer at Crewe".

So, Grandfather and Frederic Bennett had been at Crewe together after all; and had, no doubt, as my mother professed, remained friends while they both later worked in London; my grandfather at the Pall Mall & St James Electric Light Co and Frederic Bennett at his motor agency. No wonder my grandfather's elder brother, fine-waxed-moustached Great-uncle Percy, had been the proud owner of one of the first Cadillacs in England. As the reasonably affluent close relative of a friend of Frederic Bennett's, he was a natural sale. Humble pie had

175

to be eaten – in very large doses – and yet another extraordinary family link was notched up.

My mother further informed me that, during a neighbourly discussion when living on the farm in Africa, and with no other connection apart from living on adjoining farms, she had discovered that someone else had been with my grandfather at Crewe, and therefore with Frederic Bennett too. That person was none other than the father of the owner of that infamous vehicle, the Chicken Manure Special or later Motor Club Special.

All I received to my query as to why this had never before been mentioned was: "Oh, didn't I tell you?" No, in truth, I am sure she never had.

So, our impetuous mechanical foray from a decade earlier had done it again, responsible now for a continuous run of the most unlikely coincidences. It was not so much that truth was stranger than fiction as that any such string of coincidences in fiction would be thrown out as far-fetched to the extreme. I suppose, for all we knew, there could even have been a link between the bowler-hatted Frederic Bennett and the heavily-sideburned Robert Faulconer? That, though, presumably, we will never know.

As for the reactions of any of the team, Frank, Bill and Tom, all of whom I still saw quite regularly, displayed a resigned acceptance, as though such coincidences were now the norm – either that, or they were fully disbelieving and merely humouring me. On the other hand, the grandson of that third Crewe engineer, when finally tracked down, was delighted. He even answered a question I had pondered for years: what became of that magnificent transport in Africa that we had rescued from its smelly past.

Younger than me, he, it transpired, had continued the use – and the abuse – of the faithful machine just like me before him; but, the car being that much older by then, he had ended up with the short straw. All the same, majestic to the end, with its fine pointed bonnet, great chrome headlamps, twin side-mounts and flowing wings, our heroic childhood car was last seen, many years ago, rotting quietly in someone's back yard: like the University Buick, it too had finally died.

I telephoned the archivist at Beaulieu to share with him these snippets of information, unearthed with the help of the papers he had sent, and to enquire of the third item that had struck me.

In the present-day records of the Veteran Car Club, there was a 1903 Cadillac registered to a Mr Bennett. Possibly due to my excitement at the recent discoveries, he confessed that this was the very same car involved in the 1903 and 1953 thousand-mile endurance runs; and that the car in fact resided, semi-permanently on show, at the museum.

"It can't be?" I said, drawing breath, "That means after nearly a hundred years the family still own the car... and the first ever of its kind imported into England too?"

"Well, I suppose the 'Mr Bennett' *could* be a coincidence," came the reply, "but I somehow doubt it!"

"How can I get hold of this Mr. Bennett?" I enquired.

"Well, the least I can do is to give you a contact at the Veteran Car Club... they should be able to help."

The kindly lady who answered the telephone, when asked, had no intention of divulging the whereabouts, or even admitting to the existence, of any such member – regardless from where the introduction had come: club records were strictly confidential. I agreed therefore to address a letter to the elusive Mr Bennett, care of the club, which I was promised would be forwarded, "*if* such a member existed".

Early of an evening, barely a week later, I received a call: "This is Julian Bennett," a quiet, matter-of-fact voice said. Then, after a short silence: "You wrote to me."

"Yes," I blurted out, taken by surprise, "I did."

Julian 'Frederic' Bennett – in his late thirties – was Frederic Bennett's grandson and owner, along with his cousin Jill in Australia, of that original 1903 car, production No 530, complete with Leland & Faulconer engine. We chatted away, discussing how our grandfathers would chuckle at our having unexpectedly linked up. He explained the loss of contact between Bennetts and Veteran cars, due partly to his father not being as enthusiastic as his grandfather had been, and partly to the fact that the family had emigrated to Africa in the 1950s. The car had thus been left in England in the charge of others and had eventually passed to Julian and his cousin.

"Why don't we meet up?" I suggested.

"Yes, why not," he replied, "and I'll bring along some photographs and old documents that have been passed on to me."

We met up several weeks later and went off for a pub lunch. We traded stories about Africa and swapped information on the early days of our families in England. When it came to the Royal Baby Cars, Julian seemed a little startled. I took scant notice at the time and moved onto the RAC 1,000-mile Reliability Runs. After a short while, I posed a question I had been itching to ask.

"What *about* 2003?"

"What about 2003?" he queried, with a frown.

"Well, your grandfather did the original eight-day run in 1903 in No 530 and in 1953, to the hour and to the mile, he repeated it again. Apparently, so I am informed, he also did it in 1913. All the routes he took are still there and Crystal Palace Park, from where he started each day, is still very much on the map. In fact, I raced the Roadster at Crystal Palace only last year, never for a moment suspecting there was any such connection."

"Also, you are 'Frederic' as well," I went on, "as was your father before you apparently. So, what about 'Frederic III' doing a centenary run in 2003?"

He stared blankly for what seemed an age before replying: "Do you think anyone would be interested?"

"Interested? Would anyone be interested? In 1953 your grandfather ended up on television on both sides of the Atlantic. It was incredible enough to still own a car fifty years later... now we are talking about a *hundred* years... to say nothing of the fact that '530' was the first of the marque imported into the country. Much more likely that people would be incredulous," then quoting again from that sixties South African review, as I had when about to start on the Roadster, "Go on, for the sake of the show, give it a go!"

A couple of months later, after a score of e-mails – I having at last succumbed to this now user-friendly technology – Julian and I found ourselves at the RAC Club. We were there by invitation to inspect the magnificent Dewar Trophy, a cup big enough to have been photographed with Henry Leland's grandson sitting inside – the same little boy who was given one of the third-scale electric cars on his fifth birthday. Now, resplendent, in its own wall-mounted cabinet, the ornate silver cup resided at one end of the Club's colonnaded, mosaiced underground swimming pool.

While at the RAC Club, we took the opportunity to seek support for Julian's 2003 repeat of what was effectively *their* 1903 1,000-mile Reliability Trial.

"When exactly are you thinking of doing the run... and from where?" asked the club secretary.

"At eight o'clock in the morning on the 18th September from Crystal Palace," we replied, almost as one.

Julian explained that his grandfather had followed everything to the letter during each of the runs. He had even retained the same odd rear wheel that he had had to fit during the 1903 trial when run into by a steam omnibus in, of all places, Sevenoaks – the home of the motor racing club I had eventually joined.

"Oh, I see, how extraordinary," came the reply from our host with a chuckle. "In that case, we really ought somehow to be involved."

After we had left, Julian finally admitted why he had been so startled at the mention of the baby replicas. Apparently, his mother had for years been expounding tales of these little cars belonging to Queen Alexandra and the King of Siam that his grandfather had designed and had made in London. However, just as I had written off my mother's seemingly imaginary stories, Julian, just as much, had been pooh-poohing those of *his* mother. Therefore, he too was now having to eat humble pie. We laughed out aloud at the thought of us both having been caught in the same respective inter-related traps.

Meanwhile, preparations for the Grand International progressed apace. 'The Bennett Run', Julian's centennial re-run, had now become an integral part of the event; as too would a 'Grand Coach Tour' that was being organised by the club treasurer. This nine-day excursion, mainly visiting motoring spots in the south of England, was to start at Beaulieu the week before the Bennett Run and end at the Show on the Saturday.

'The Show' in Crystal Palace Park, under the direction of the Show Organiser would be the prime event, to be held in the very spot where the contestants of the 1903 Endurance Trial had set forth and returned each day all that time ago.

Thus, as we headed into year two of the Millennium, a serious challenge loomed: would 530, inactive for two decades or more sitting in the Beaulieu Motor Museum, be up to completing a gruelling 1,000 miles in eight days under the same rules and over the same routes as in 1903?

Whether or not we harboured any doubts as to the wisdom of taking on such a challenge, at least the Veteran Car Club, for all its initial secrecy, had now agreed to provide daily observers and produce a similar authentication certificate to one issued by them in 1953. At this, confidence rising to the fore, we rushed headlong into yet another Lion's Den.

16. A 'Grand' Plan

"You and Julian will be alright organising the Bennett Run, won't you," the club chairman declared, after which someone added, "We'll concentrate on the Coach Tour and the Show itself. That'll be OK, won't it?"

Somehow, the finger was pointing rather too much at me. The club's long-time show organiser and his regular team of helpers should have no difficulty with the show on the Run's 'rest day', originally a Sunday but this time a Saturday, and the treasurer was organising the Coach Tour with outside professionals. Julian and I, on the other hand, would be attempting to arrange a once-in-fifty-years one-off run, and with no one around from 1953 to help or advise.

A couple of non-committee members, possibly out of sympathy, offered to help. One, a wizard in graphic design and computer technology, and the other, a pool of much needed down-to-earth common sense. Fortunately, they both appeared to see the event as a once-off opportunity not to be missed.

First off, we needed to know the return routes travelled to the eight towns during the original 1903 Trial and, if possible, some idea of the rules prevailing; to say nothing of what Frederic Bennett had done on his 1953 run. So, back to the old contacts: the RAC Club and Beaulieu Motor Museum.

Both came up trumps: from the RAC, we received the official report and relevant rules together with some interesting pictures and, from Beaulieu, we received the original route map along with page-upon-page from 'Autocar' magazine of September and October 1903. These described in detail what had transpired all that time ago, even an official observer's list of 'pet hates'. In descending order, these were, *dust, early rising, sitting still all day, police traps, dogs, pigs, cattle, lady cyclists, and small boys*. Apart from the dust, pigs and cattle, we noted that not a lot had changed!

As for sponsors, the American Club was quick to chip in. Due to the Dot Com crash, though, corporate sponsors took a bit more cajoling; but, in the end, did steadily come on line, as did the necessary follow-up vehicles and drivers. The follow-ups would travel behind

Julian as protection, while a support vehicle would be needed to drive ahead seeing the way was clear as well as to look after the daily preparations. The Roadster, which we hoped would add to the general PR, was quickly designated Official Support Vehicle and the self-professed Back-up of old was requested – in as serious a note as any 'boys only' occasion might warrant – to do the backing up once more. Her somewhat muted affirmative was taken as a fully-fledged "yes".

As luck had it, the London Fine Art & Antiques Fair, having heard what we were up to, asked to use Julian and 530 as a theme for their Summer Fair being held at London Olympia. Such a prestigious show could hardly have been a better launch pad.

Then, out of the blue, the German Club, having also decided to add to the sponsorship, sent in a photograph taken sometime in the early nineteen-fifties of Stirling Moss, that great enduring motor racing ace, sitting in 530 alongside Frederic Bennett. A note accompanying the picture stated that "Sir Frederic and Sir Stirling" had been discovered in a book belonging to one of their members.

We wrote back thanking them for their welcome input, while pointing out that, sadly, Mr Bennett had never gained the 'Sir' and that Sir Stirling had received his many years after the picture was taken. I immediately telephoned Julian.

"Did you know that there's a photo of Stirling Moss and your grandfather sitting together in 530 sometime back in the fifties?" I asked.

"Oh, yes," he replied, quite unmoved, "I have a whole lot of those," adding, after a pause, "Didn't I show you them?"

No, he had most certainly not shown them to me.

"Julian, what do you mean, 'you have a whole lot of them'? Where do they come from... what was it about?"

"Well," he continued, in his typically nonchalant way, "the two of them did the London to Brighton Run together in 1952, the year before the 1953 Run. There are some news articles about it too somewhere."

I could barely believe it: here we were trying to organise – and raise funds for – a major centennial function, and the main player omits to inform us that one of the best known motor racing icons of all time had been involved with the main object of our concern.

On receiving the other photographs of Stirling and Frederic

182

Bennett – as well as several of the great comedian George Formby from another London to Brighton Run – one or two depicted Stirling actually driving 530. Having already arranged that the Run would be in aid of BEN, the Motor and Allied Trades Benevolent Fund, of which Julian's grandfather had been a life-long supporter and one-time president, it so happened that Sir Stirling Moss was a BEN supporter too. Here, possibly, was an opportunity for some added PR.

Our man from the Standard, although retired from his full-time journalistic commitments, was still very much in the newspaper world but now as a freelance.

"What would be the reaction," I asked, "of a major newspaper to a couple of Moss-Bennett pictures: one of a young Stirling Moss driving an elderly Mr Bennett in a 50-year-old car, and another of Sir Stirling Moss, fifty years later, driving the same car alongside a young Mr Bennett... young Mr Bennett being elderly Mr Bennett's grandson?"

His brief silence, no doubt due to my convoluted dissertation, was followed by: "I think one of the senior papers would fall for that, and would give it good coverage too. Why, can you arrange something?"

"I don't know, but we can try," I replied.

"Who? What?" Sir Stirling part stammered, as I tried to explain a occurrence in his life from half a century earlier. Then, a little more jovially: "Oh, I know who you mean," then, lightening up further still, "Yes, I remember him well, he was a very nice man. Yes, all right, I'll get back to you with a date for a photo-shoot... but it will have to be here, in London, if that's all right."

Yes, of course it was all right; but how, after my natural concern at contacting the great racing ace, could it all have been so disbelievingly simple.

Stirling, as promised, got back to us with a date, so we set up a joint photo-shoot with the Fine Art & Antiques Fair. When the day came, it either poured with rain, drizzled or, at the very least, the black clouds continued to hang menacingly overhead. We arrived at Stirling's front door at ten o'clock as agreed to be welcomed by the great man himself. We were ushered into his inner sanctum with far greater courtesy than we warranted, whereupon we produced the pictures from fifty years earlier.

"Wait there," Stirling said, disappearing from the room.

Wait we did, admiring the array of mementos and photographs of a truly extraordinary and glamorous international career.

"Look," he said, as he returned, prising open a large plastic bag with some heavy-looking garment inside, "I think this is the one." To which, as he pulled the overcoat free and began looking for the label, I irreverently chipped in: "Surely, you haven't got the date in there, have you?"

"Yes," he said, "look, here it is... November 1953! Will that do?"

"Two months too young," was my reflex and equally irreverent remark. To which Stirling looked up, smiled and declared: "Well, shall I wear it anyway?"

"Yes," we attested in unison and, while chatting about Bennetts past and present, we headed outside together into the narrowest of narrow London streets to attempt a photo-shoot.

We more than mildly hindered the traffic, although no one seemed to mind and, while Stirling waved and gesticulated to all around, to which most waved back and many wished him well, we clicked away, professional and amateur alike. I guess we behaved like a bunch of kids – well, professional amateur sort of kids, while enjoying ourselves immensely – and Stirling certainly enjoyed meeting the amenable grandson of the well-remembered equally amenable grandfather.

In the end, much to my continued irritation with the wonders of computer technology, the only usable pictures were from a not-too-special digital camera by the non-professionals. Somehow, this ultra-modern computerised gadget, with all its electronic calculations, managed to sort out the light and the colours that no ordinary camera, professional or otherwise, seemed able to do. Memories of computerised windscreen-wiper actuation and complete car body design flooded back.

Before leaving, an ever-helpful Stirling asked what else he could do to assist with the Run.

"Would you," we asked, "be prepared to come to our Show on the rest day?"

After checking his diary: "Yes, certainly," he declared.

We agreed to talk before the Show, then departed, 530 in tow, with more smiles, handshakes and waves all around.

The involvement of Sir Stirling Moss was to put an entirely new dimension on the event. No sooner had the information leaked than stories appeared in a number of magazines and, as assured, two articles in a top daily newspaper. However, even before the first article had appeared, suggestions and ideas poured in from friends and club members alike.

"Why not ask GM in the US for financial backing... it would be great PR for them?" and "Why not get the mayors or somebody famous from all the end-towns to meet Frederic III when he arrives?" then, to top it, "Why not get the BBC to film it, just like they did in 1953... they would love it?"

We did approach GM for support but, at Julian's insistence and with the club's agreement, the Run itself, as always before, would be strictly a club and family affair. Instead, we asked GM for something rather different: would they fund the transportation and care of the Queen Alexandra/Prince Olaf Baby Cadillac from Norway to London for the duration of the event.

After their disbelief – not surprisingly – at what the eccentric British were up to now, they did eventually relent. Indeed, not only did they concede to paying for the third-scale replica car's transportation and care, they also agreed to fund a quality commemorative brochure for the Grand International as well as throwing in some extra to help with the celebrations.

We then wrote to the nine prospective mayors; eight covering the end-towns where Julian, God willing, would be arriving each day and the Mayor of Bromley, who covered Crystal Palace. While the end-town mayors would be required to meet Julian during the lunchtime turn-arounds, the Mayor of Bromley would have to be at the Queens Hotel, Crystal Palace, at 7.30am on the first day for the 'off'.

The Hotel, where Frederic Bennett had royally ensconced himself in 1953, was the perfect backdrop for the present challenge – Julian having turned up yet more photographs taken here too. On close inspection, we realised that most of the hotel, built in the 1850s to accommodate the great and the good visiting the Crystal Palace itself, was much unchanged even from 1903, let alone 1953.

As for the BBC having filmed the end of the Run in 1953, there was only a single black & white photograph of this and no one knew when, how or on what program it had been shown.

Then, one morning, not long after our sending out the mayoral letters, I received a call from the secretary of the Club: "There's this fellow been on the line saying something about having GM's dossier on the 1953 Bennett Run. Do you know what he's talking about... or anything about it?"

Having replied in the negative, the secretary continued: "Anyway, he left me a number, so you'd best ring him and see what it's about."

I did: and "this fellow", Bob Monro, was in possession of just what he said. His father had worked for GM and had rescued the seventy-page dossier from the rubbish tip when they were having a clear out. Compiled by a London agency, the priceless documentation of the 1953 Run, most of which was press reports and press releases, had been prepared on the instructions of GM UK, apparently quite unknown by anyone else, either then or now.

Of greatest interest, was an entry on page fifteen, stating: *29th September – BBC TV Service, 4-minute News Film – 4,500,000 approx viewers' estimate at time of programme.* Amazingly, just when we needed it, here was the answer to the when and where of the 1953 TV item. Was there, though, any possibility that such a recording still existed?

The BBC archives had to be the first port of call. Still, this was fifty years on and TV back then was in its infancy. I was passed from one person to another until, having explained my request for the fourth time and after a protracted wait, I was about to give up. Then, suddenly: "Yes, here it is," stated a soft, lightly singing voice, "It was on the National News."

After my expletive of surprise, the kindly voice continued: "Well, as there is a family member involved, I'm sure I can let you have a copy for a token fee... but it must not be used commercially under any circumstances."

I unhesitatingly agreed, gave the necessary details and thanked the benevolent archivist as profusely as I knew. "Yes, here it is!" It was like walking over a grave: just as had been said about the Faulconer discovery. When the video arrived, there, chatting to a BBC presenter – in front of a very recognisable Queens Hotel – was a sprightly nearly eighty-year-old Frederic Bennett. When asked by the presenter whether he would be doing the Run again in fifty years time, he simply said, while letting out a muted chuckle and sporting a beaming smile, "I hope so!". Julian, having often wondered about his grandfather, was about to see and hear him in action for the first time – that, for sure, had to be really spooky.

Frederic III had already been on local radio and had attended a couple of press days at the Fine Arts & Antiques Fair. Therefore, knowing now that the BBC possessed a 50-year-old news item from a Golden Jubilee Run, we informed their present-day newsrooms of the Centennial Run. The bait was taken and BBC South put out a preview on their evening news a week before the off, promising to contact us again during the Run itself.

Of growing concern, though, was the fact that Julian had barely managed fifty miles in 530 since, as Julian explained, being "set right" by a specialist restorer. "Set right" she might have been, but other problems had emerged. For one, 530's very basic carburettor had needed some hard-to-come-by parts, which, eventually, were sourced across the Atlantic through 'Mr Single Cylinder', as the expert in these ancient Veterans is affectionately known. In fact, on hearing that Julian was doing the Run for charity, he refused any payment. More support like that of old was, as always, well received and much appreciated.

Meanwhile, the wizard in graphic design and computer technology, having already produced a promotional brochure, had set up "Guess the Miles" and "Guess the Speed" on a website in all of four languages as a way of helping raise money for BEN. This would be open until the 'off' and, thereafter, each evening, he would update the site to keep the donors abreast of the likely correctness of their guessability.

While checking final arrangements, two statements kept cropping up with monotonous regularity, both of which we dreaded: the one was, "Don't worry, sir, it will all be alright", in a sort of singing positive tone; and the other was, "It's the Mayor's Secretary here." When the first occurred, whoever was involved immediately noted that another telephone call would likely be required and, with the second, considering the number of mayors, we simply remained silent, hoping that the caller would give some hint as to which. Both, fortunately, seemed to work.

In the end, incredibly, all nine mayors agreed to participate. We deduced from this, with great satisfaction, that there must be some universal, non-motoring appeal to this unusual human, but very motoring event.

Farmer Frank, as so often, came up with one of his typical man-of-the-land concerns: "What happens," he said, "if that ancient rickety little old car decides, as likely as not, to die on one of the daily runs. What are those be-chained dignitaries going to think when you don't turn up?"

Without waiting for an answer, he promptly offered the use of his car-transporter for the duration of the Run. So, the greatest sceptic of them all came up trumps and solved at a stroke a very real potential problem; although we dearly hoped his generosity would go unused.

All the same, the likely performance of 530, with its hand throttle, adjustable ignition and foot operated gears, which, together with the brake, seemed to require at least three hands and both feet to operate, was anyone's guess. We were now within days of the start and, even with the cured carburettor, Julian had still only managed to cover less than a hundred miles.

Apart from this, the owner of the Queens Hotel, on discovering that the baby car about to grace his establishment was a *Royal* car, insisted it be on full display in the main entrance, rather than in the ballroom as originally agreed. The fact that the only access to the foyer was up the grand 1850's steps, and that the car with its glass case weighed many hundreds of pounds, seemed not to bother him at all.

"It will take a *great* number of people to carry it up the steps," I said, with all the concern I could muster.

To which, he simply replied: "I *employ* a great number of people," and, smiling benignly, suggested we get on to the next item on the agenda of our one and only meeting.

None of us were best pleased with this turn of events; especially as the item in question was only due to arrive on the eve of the Run. Still, there seemed little option but to comply – the hotel was allowing a string of concessions, none of which we wished to jeopardise.

Meanwhile, the Roadster, no doubt to keep its end up in the face of the intensifying competition, had gained a dubious but unique distinction. Our neo-classic, as described by one magazine, had become the first car to notch up a second outright win of the Annual Concourse at our local Coln Valley Car Club. That said, the bestowing of such an honour could easily be seen as an unseemly mistake, not once but twice.

On the first occasion, the representative of a recipient charity was asked to do the honours and act as judge. Nobody, however, thought to inform the most charming and eloquent lady that the Roadster was not all it appeared. The result was met with stunned silence, numerous long faces and the Roadster's keeper having to be extricated from the bar to receive the trophy. Now, on this second occasion, when the official judge failed to turn up, the manager of the 'club's pub' was asked to choose which of the antique icons scattered around his car park he would most like to take home. In strict contrast to the first, the resultant win evoked much laughter, numerous cheers and drinks all round: a welcome change indeed.

Of less questionable honour was what took place a short time later at the home town's bi-annual industrial exhibition. The keeper of the FA Cup, there as part of the PR, spying the Roadster during a break in the football banter, demanded a photo-shoot with "Cup and pretty ladies with all that gleaming chrome". Being the original 1908 cup with its well-worn baize base, the resulting scratches on the bonnet – be they very faint – are still there, proudly left for all to see. Such, it would appear, is the desire for all and any fame.

Then, while discussing final arrangements for Stirling's visit to the Grand Event, Lady Moss became quite definite: "No, don't encourage him," she said at my suggestion of testing the Roadster on the remains of Crystal Palace racetrack, quickly adding: "Remember, these Mosses are all very competitive... personally, I think the two of you should be kept well apart!"

As Stirling in his earlier years had often competed on Crystal Palace racetrack, I thought the idea might well amuse him. Still, to keep the peace, I sort-of concurred.

At least the Grand Coach Tour was going smoothly. The guests had all arrived safely and spent the first two days at the annual Beaulieu Autojumble. This had been followed during the week with excursions to various museums and other places of motoring note, culminating in the private viewing of the Dewar Trophy in the RAC Club in Pall Mall; at which, one and all from the other side of the Atlantic, admitted that not *everything* was bigger and better in America.

When the time came to off-load the Queen Alexandra/Prince Olaf Baby Cadillac on a fine windless morning the day before the start, our earlier fears were more than justified. Having arrived tied to the forward end of the cavernous rear of its own special Scandinavian transport – a lorry as large as the car was small – the one-third scale model was completely obscured by a mass of exhibition paraphernalia destined for the lorry's return journey.

While littering the hotel entrance with this together with an assortment of packaging materials, I asked the driver what he would have done had it been raining: "Ya, vell... but it dose-ent happen... so vhy vorry."

"Yes, of course," I replied, wondering whether the remark bode well for its natural common sense or badly for its casualness. At the same time, and for no apparent reason, someone half-glowering half-smiling, tugged at my shirtsleeve.

"What?" I asked, slightly taken aback at having been interrupted by a young man who had appeared from nowhere along with a group of others now milling aimlessly around the forecourt.

"Cum... us help!" and I was ushered towards the group.

Slowly, it dawned: these were "I employ a lot of people". My heart sank: they were all obviously from Eastern Europe and none of them appeared to speak a word of English; and we were supposed, in a co-ordinated and disciplined way, to be carrying a valuable museum exhibit up twelve steps rising some eight feet from the drive below.

We soon discovered that the other half of the "I employ a lot of people", while speaking reasonable English, comprised of a large over-weight and obviously not very fit chef, several of his kitchen staff, a security guard approaching seventy, the manager who was barely five feet tall, his spindly deputy and, finally, a long-standing local groundsman who saw the whole likely fiasco as that week's entertainment. At this, understandably, my heart sank further.

Having untied and, with a portable forklift, wheeled the Royal Baby Car and its case along the truck's length onto the electric tail-lift, and thus to the ground, I noticed the driver was in deep and concerned conversation with my down-to-earth common sense colleague who had arrived all the way from Yorkshire.

"What's he saying?" I enquired, as I approached.

"He says you must have underestimated the weight. He can tell from the effort he has to apply to the fork-lift's jacking system that it weighs nearly a thousand pounds."

"One thousand pounds!" I exclaimed in disbelief, "He must be kidding. Even with its batteries... which have been left in Norway... the little car is only supposed to weigh just over four hundred pounds. Also, the museum has swapped the glass for lighter-weight Perspex. What on earth is the case made of?"

I received no reply: save for a fixed stare from my colleague and a partly hidden grin from the groundsman. For the rest, there were blank faces all around.

The driver was right. The case's decorative wooden base was merely a facade; beneath was a mass of indestructible steel, as was the framework supporting the Perspex. Those delightfully pedantic Norwegians had built the case in true battleship style, just as Lionel had said we had done with the internal structure of the Roadster.

In truth, as with those university stories of old that had surreptitiously jabbed at me while constructing the Roadster: we should have checked and double-checked. Moreover, we should have demanded, there and then, as originally agreed, that the so-called 'little' car be ensconced in the ballroom with its ground-level drive-in access. Rightly or wrongly, we did not.

"OK, what now?" I enquired of nobody in particular, while forcing some pretence at looking intelligent in a fairly unintelligent situation.

"Look, over there," interjected my colleague, "There's a whole lot of scaffold poles and connectors... someone's been doing some painting... why not build a framework out of that and then get some more hands to join in."

A brainwave of old: yes, why not. Then turning to the manager: "Can you muster up a total of ... say... twenty staff?"

"Oo, sir... that could be being very difficult now, sir,"

"Your Owner," I said, with a certain air of what I considered well-warranted authority, "wanted the car in the foyer. You were there when he said, *'I employ a lot of people'*, so please go and *somehow* find *'a lot of people'*."

"Sir, I can only be doing my best... and for you and this beautiful little car, I will be doing my best."

He was as good as his word. While the rest of us assembled the scaffolding with a plethora of "don't touch!" and "leave that alone" aimed at one particularly overenthusiastic helper, the ever-smiling manager turned out several cleaners and a brace of bedroom attendants. Then, with car and case well anchored to the scaffolding, and under the watchful eye of the Scandinavian deliverer, who had long since proved that common sense rather than casualness prevailed, some twenty men and boys – nationalities ranging from American to Asian through European and African – began manhandling the not-insubstantial car up the hotel steps on our hastily-rigged bed of scaffold poles.

Barely a third of the way up, case and car began, gradually, to teeter sideways and settle at the rear; from which point I was attempting – as my colleague likewise up front – to direct the operations in some orderly manner. As I quickly added my efforts to the lifting, I saw, with a twinge of horror, that the little car was only resting on and not tied to the axle-stands protruding from the base of its case, and that four-hundred-plus pounds of vehicle was on the verge of coming adrift.

There was no going backwards, and the thought of a ninety-year-old one of only three crashing through the Perspex and careering across the hotel car park and out under the entrance arch into a main London road was more than I cared to contemplate – to say nothing of the possibility of its running me over on the way. Galvanised by such thoughts, I shouted out in broken English, explaining the problem as best I could. Then, in desperation, realising the lack of comprehension of many of the 'heavers to', my colleague and I began a chant:

"*Up! Up!*" we shouted. "*Up! Up!*" they chanted back. Again and again we cajoled, keeping the *"Up! Up!"* rhythm up, and slowly, but ever so surely, the back began to lift, the sideways tilt gradually shifted towards the upright, and we moved on up a step. Then again, with several more *"Up! Ups!"* the unlikely procession added yet another step or two. Another pause, another tilt, and yet another fear; even worse as I glanced behind me, now two-thirds up, and saw the steep descent to the driveway below growing ever greater.

Repeatedly chanting all the way, we carried on step by steady step. Then, one last chant and we were at the top, outside the hotel entrance double-doors. *"Down! Down!* but slowly mind," and down she slowly went – the worst, at last, was over. The *"Ups!"* and the *"Downs!"* were immediately replaced by singing, muscle bearing, the odd jig and numerous arguments as to who had helped the most.

Understandably, a well-earned rest followed. After which, with great ingenuity and without breaking or marking any part of the beautifully preserved Royal Toy or its protection, we eased case and car through the double-doors and placed them, facing outwards, in the lobby – just as the insistent owner had requested.

When the explanatory graphics had been mounted on the surrounding walls, a well-deserved celebration ensued. Yes, mad British we may have been, but this time it had been a truly international mad affair.

Later in the day, when 530 was over two hours late, the waiting team were beyond caring – after such a morning's interlude, we just shrugged our shoulders and lingered in the bar. When she did eventually arrive and had been de-trailered, 530 was simply put to bed in the coach-house, specially reserved for her, the Roadster and a great 1930's V16 due to arrive all the way from Jersey the following day. We retired to bed, ever mindful of the next morning's early and all-important start.

As my head met the pillow, I wondered whether we were remotely intelligent in attempting such a challenge: a Veteran car was endeavouring to complete something that had been hard enough when brand new, let alone when fifty, and now a hundred-years-old. Still, too late to call a halt now.

17. Rare Challenge

Thursday, 18th September 2003: one hundred years to the day that the contestants in the 1903 Reliability Trial had assembled in Crystal Palace Park, and fifty years since Frederic Bennett had set out on his Golden Jubilee re-run. Here we were, bright and sparky, once more outside the Queens Hotel and on a glorious late summer's morning.

The Coach Tour arrived as expected at seven for breakfast and the mayoral entourage appeared on time at seven-thirty. The late arrival of the BBC, who thought that twenty minutes in the morning rush hour was reasonable travelling time from the M25 to Crystal Palace, was only a minor blip. Everyone joined in with handshakes, congratulations and questions, along with admiring glances at the spectacular little car in the foyer – if only they had been there the previous day.

After an official oration by the Mayor from the hotel steps, Julian and 530, together with his navigator for the first two days, and closely followed by the follow-up vehicle, left for Margate, that day's destination. Shortly afterwards, we, the official support team in the Roadster, headed off in pursuit. For each of the Trial days, we would be travelling outbound on the old roads that 530 was set to use, then, after meeting up with the town's reception committee and doing whatever else was needed, we would return by the fastest routes possible to prepare for 530's homecoming.

On this first morning, as we came up behind the two-car convoy a mile or so ahead, we could see the bright yellow follow-up vehicle, with its flashing amber light for added protection, trailing the little all-black 530. Together, they headed up an orderly procession of cars and trucks wending their way into the countryside. When chance permitted, one by one, the followers would pull out and overtake, leaving the leisurely unlikely duo plodding on behind.

530 performed reasonably well outbound; apart, that is, from a number of mudguard-fixing bolts that flew off into the road with clock-setting regularity – not the car's fault, just bad decorative substitutes fitted sometime during the car's not-so-eventful life since the 1953 Run. Stopping at a lawn-mower repairer in search of suitable replacements, the staff came tumbling out to inspect the unexpected

while the poor unfortunate manager, single-handedly, attempted to locate what was needed within.

Partly due to London traffic and partly due to the hold-ups, our timing was badly out. We, the official support team, found ourselves wandering the streets of Margate on a personally guided tour by a fully-robed, fully-bechained Mayor. After which, on reaching the Mayor's Parlour, the mayoral staff set about packing 'doggie bags' for 530 and crew. The waiting media, meanwhile, were left admiring the view and chatting to passers-by in Margate's Cecil Square. Eventually, some two hours late, they managed to fill notepads and reels of film.

The return was equally eventful: arriving at the top of Detling Hill rather faster than the occupants would have wished, 530 descended the long tortuous incline at ever-increasing speed. Having tried the brakes to little effect, Julian declined to use his grandfather's emergency of engaging reverse. As they continued their headlong rush, the navigator, adrenalin rising ever higher while silently clinging to the back of his open, belt-less seat, claimed to have been nearer his maker than ever before or than ever he wished again. "Coming down Detling Hill at 40mph," he spluttered on his return, "felt more like 140mph!" Miraculously, the road ahead was clear.

Viewing the inadequacies from the comfort of the follow-up vehicle, that day's Veteran Car Club observer expressed horror at the apparent lack of preparation, to say nothing of the almost complete absence of any tools, and reported back accordingly to his Club. That said, he offered a string of invaluable advice and made us painfully aware of the many hazards that lay ahead.

To add to that first day's problems, the specially invited ex-Maharajah's sixteen-cylindered 1931 Cadillac arrived at the Queens Hotel without a proper welcome. On our eventual return and after introductions were complete, rooms checked and luggage offloaded, we were forgiven our indiscretion; and the giant of a car's somewhat lesser-sized owner – but of no lesser presence – parked the colossal open tourer in the coach-house.

Later, as the hill-descending navigator brought 530 through the old coach-house doors, adrenalin still pumping, I casually said: "Whatever you do, *don't* hit the V16," Then, in jest, added, "Just aim at the Roadster." To which, flooring some pedal or other, he placed 530's front spring shackle square in the middle of the Roadster's rear-end, leaving a crumpled number-plate and a nasty dent in its curvaceous tail. Having again used that nerve-calming statement of, "Don't worry, it's only a piece of metal," to some small effect, we put the unfortunate mishap behind us and joined the others.

Early the following morning, I headed for the coach-house to survey the damage to the Roadster. Although not a pretty sight, at least the official support vehicle was useable: we had endured enough jests of how funny it would be if the Roadster was unable to complete the course and Frank's so-described "little old antique" did.

After nervously directing the V16 out over a nasty piece of protruding concrete, I started up the Roadster. I put her into reverse and headed out, still mulling over the damage and wondering what Gavin would make of his un-prettied handiwork. Scscscsc! I stopped. The chassis rubbing on that concrete slab, I assumed: I put my foot down a little harder. Crack! followed by Roar! was followed by my foot's instant swap from accelerator to brake. I sat there, bewildered.

Gradually, reality dawned: what a fool. In my ongoing concern for the Roadster's rear-end, I had caught the left-hand exhaust manifold on the vertical edge of the concrete slab and snapped the cast-iron outlet clean off. We had always known the Seville was no off-roader: that was now proved good and true.

As I sat there, a little stunned, I decided with a twinge of irritation that 530's attack on the Roadster the previous evening was really to blame. Was it jealousy: had the Roadster received too much attention in Margate and now 530 wanted the field to itself? That any car could have a mind of its own is beyond doubt; but, like it or not, this was no five-minute repair and the official support vehicle was off the road for the duration. Yes, laugh they could: the Roadster out of the game on day two; and 530, at that very moment, chug chug chugging up the slope from the coach-house, was still going strong.

Much to my humiliation and with a certain continuing irritation, one elderly Chevrolet Caprice, much akin to a Californian police car, would be taking over as support vehicle instead.

After an official flag-waving start by the V16's septuagenarian owner – the 'Maharajah', as he soon become known – 530 was soon trundling along in the morning rush hour on the way to Eastbourne. Soon also, did the replacement support vehicle, its driver continuing to mull over his foolishness, manage to get lost, both while leaving

London and getting into Eastbourne.

Meanwhile, the Grand Coach Tour, whose dedicated mission that morning was to tag Julian to his seaside destination, had an equally erratic trip. As reported by that day's Veteran Car Club observer: *"Sitting in comfort in the follow-up vehicle, I had time to recall the antics of the late Benny Hill. Julian would stop every twenty minutes or so to attend to 530's needs, at which a large coach pulled alongside, disgorging its human cargo, cameras at the ready. Julian would then bring 530 to life and set off again, leaving the occupants of the coach clamouring to get back on board. I somehow began to see it all in fast motion – it would have made a great comedy."*

Eventually, the tour leader, exasperated by the Benny Hill antics, to say nothing of his desire to return his charges in one piece to the bosom of their families, directed the coach driver to make straight for the Eastbourne meeting point. To counter our joint late arrival, the diminutive, elderly Lady Mayor had already been taken for a seafront ride in an open 'plushmobile' that had joined the day's following.

"Is there any news of the Bennett car?" she enquired, as we stood waiting patiently for 530's chug, chug, chug, which had eventually alerted us to its late arrival in Cecil Square the previous day.

"They seemed to be going fine last time we spoke," I replied, then added, "They did have to stop to adjust the fuel mixture and they did say something about an overheating problem... nothing too serious, though. I'll give them another call."

"Who's that?" I enquired, when a vaguely recognisable voice answered the follow-up car's mobile. On hearing it was the Maharajah and why he had answered – the reasoning for which was a little dubious – I continued: "Where are you? What's going on?"

"We're on the outskirts of town," he replied, "Julian and the others are up ahead doing something to the water-pump. Something has come adrift... I think I'd better go and help."

Knowing from discussions the previous evening that the Maharajah, although an internationally acclaimed engineer, was not particularly up on veteran cars, and that the Veteran Car Club observer – who most definitely was – might not brook any interference, I saw the possibility of solving two problems in one.

"No, leave them be, you're needed here. Please bring your great beast of a V16 down to the seafront... as soon as possible. The press are talking of leaving within minutes and the Mayor doesn't look like waiting around too much longer either!"

At the mention of "Press" and "Mayor", I received an immediate affirmative – the Maharajah, although casually attired in tee-shirt and baseball cap for his late summer jaunt, was never averse to a bit of fun, nor a little publicity too.

I made my way over to the waiting press: "Would you," I asked of he who was holding pad and pencil, "like to see the only 1930s ex-Maharajah's V16 open tourer ever to have been in this country?"

Initial wide eyed and questioning was followed by an excited: "Yes, where... when?"

"Here, in ten or fifteen minutes," I replied.

I then quickly headed off in the direction of the Mayor who, while ably attended by others of the Support team, was looking a little restive.

"Would you," I enquired, using the politest intonations possible, "like a ride around Eastbourne in the only ex-Maharajah's 1930s V16 open tourer ever to visit England?"

"Oh, yes please!" was followed by instructions to the mayoral aid to inform all concerned that the Mayor would be running a late that afternoon.

When the Maharajah arrived, the news he brought was not good:

the water-pump, itself one of only two mechanical items to have caused trouble in 1953, was now mortally ill. Its internal impeller had broken loose from the drive-shaft and any repair would take rather longer than at first thought.

"Don't worry," he whispered with a chuckle, before clambering back into his mighty steed and pulling himself up behind the wheel, "I'll *capture* the Mayor until 530 arrives!"

After persuading an ever-thickening crowd to pull back from a barely visible V16, the Maharajah set off with the Mayor well ensconced in the sumptuous leather rear.

No sooner had they left, than a call from out of town informed us that all was far from well: the water-pump drive-shaft had not merely come adrift, it had broken and was quite unrepairable.

So this was the end of the challenge and so soon; and *before* the following day's show rather than, less embarrassingly, *after* it. Poor Julian, what bad luck: and for all of us too for that matter. To end like this after everyone had put in so much work was a bitter pill indeed.

I then remembered that it was on this very day in 1903, after the catastrophe of having been run into by the steam omnibus in Sevenoaks, that Grandfather Frederic had so nearly been put out of the original Trial. Yet he had gone to the most extraordinary lengths to continue, rushing to London and back by train to obtain the odd wheel that was still on the car to this day; and eventually finishing the Trial by winning in his class. Could we now give up where he had battled on, especially while nearly nine hours remained before the midnight deadline as laid down in the 1903 rules?

However, if by some miraculous chance we were able to get 530 back on the road and return to Crystal Palace before the bewitching hour, thereby resurrecting the Run, there would be a missing authenticating mayoral photograph. Also, how could we help encourage the other half of the team trying to find some way of repairing an irreparable pump? A little urgent conferring soon produced one of those brainwaves of old.

As the Mayor returned and alighted from the regal surroundings, I posed the question: "Would you by any chance be prepared to drive to the edge of town and do a photo-shoot with Mr Bennett... in the car alongside the road?"

Having, so it appeared, thoroughly enjoyed the ride, she paused, smiled and turned to her mayoral aid to enquire of *his* willing.

"Certainly, your worship," he answered, with a smile to match; and, without further thought, they headed for the mayoral limousine to make their way out of town. We followed, leaving the Maharajah to enjoy the ever-growing re-emerging crowd.

At sight of the Mayor, chain of office still in place, the Bennett party stared, a trifle disbelieving. It had the desired effect: not only did we get that all-important mayoral photograph but the two engineers, who had been summoned by the Veteran Car Club observer, concluded this must be rather more important an affair than at first they thought.

There were no more "maybes" or "tomorrows". They removed the offending pump, headed off to their workshop nearby, rebuilt the pump by fabricating a completely new shaft from scratch and were back on hand by five-thirty. Then, while a willing local householder supplied hose and water, the true saviours, legs spewed from under 530, put everything back together again. Amazingly, the aged machine was back on the road shortly after six.

While the representative for BEN, the motor trades charity, dedicated to the last, went in search of supplements to the un-filled gas headlamps, Julian and his followers drove quickly into Eastbourne to qualify for that day's run. Once there, they turned tail and headed for London as speedily as possible, both humanly and mechanically, in the now fast-fading light.

Soon after ten that evening, the triumphant procession, 530 – adorned with an assortment of battery-powered bicycle lamps attached by a multitude of cable-ties – the follow-up and the BEN vehicle, arrived back at the Queens Hotel. By the time the necessary checks had been made, everybody fed, photographs downloaded and the website updated, it was nearly two in the morning. Against all odds, the Run was back on course.

After the Show on the Saturday, the Sunday start time to Worthing was brought forward half an hour, as were subsequent day's runs. Yet, with London still fast asleep at seven-thirty on a Sunday morning, the journey proved far faster than anyone expected and we were in Worthing nearly a full hour early. Being the weekend, Julian's two teenage sons took turns at navigating – practice for 2053 perhaps?

Along with the Mayor and his wife and the waiting press, Julian was greeted by someone who had seen his grandfather arrive in 1953. He described the earlier happenings he had witnessed as a child, even where Frederic I, all those years ago, had stopped, waited, talked to well-wishers and then turned for home. So, as the 2003 convoy turned for home, he joined in to wish the grandson and great-grandsons a centennial success equal to that of the grandfather's golden jubilee.

At the end of the day, heading up the long steep hill to Crystal Palace, the engine began to play up. Car and crew eventually made it to the top, only to discover that over-oiling of the drip-feeders had fouled the ignition and produced excessive carbon build-up in the cylinder. This was causing an increase in compression, thereby making it extremely difficult to turn the engine over on the starting handle. Another potential disaster was staring us in the face.

Many hands set to de-carboning the upper areas of the cylinder and the top of the piston through the small hole into which fitted the anti-quated ignition electrodes. This was followed by a massive de-oiling and the adjustment of the automatic oilers according to the handbook in Julian's possession. When done, confidence began to build again. As someone said, it was "three down and five to go".

The next leg, to Folkestone, on another sunlit morn, saw 530 attack a poor little French car at a traffic light. The owner, on being told of Julian's quest, declined to pursue the matter. He considered it an honour, he said, to have been minorly marked by such a famous car. I suppose, on reflection, I should have felt the same about 530's unprovoked lunge at the Roadster several days earlier. Still, minorly marked was one thing, a dirty great indentation to Gavin's flowing aluminium was, in all reasonableness, quite another.

We arrived at Folkestone's Grand Hotel – in front of which the contestants had met in 1903 – to find members of the local car club out in force. Some seemed to view Frederic III as a modern-day motoring folk hero and, after much jollity and exchanges of stories, Julian had a mite trouble extracting himself from one or two of them; but, in time, extract himself he did.

Meanwhile, the owner of the Grand had laid on a Mayoral buffet in the conservatory overlooking the expanse of lawns and pristine flowerbeds, and beyond out to sea. This was the very glass-fronted enclave in which King Edward VII and his friends used regularly to meet and, bearded as they all were then and being visible from the road below, the locals had named it the 'Monkey House'. So we sat and dined in the Monkey House, admiring the splendour of the once royal view.

With speeches and pleasantries over, we headed back in excellent spirits, the bright sunlight lasting long enough for the support vehicle to whisk itself back along the motorway. Julian and his week-two navigator, though, were less fortunate. Caught in a sudden downpour, they returned looking like a couple of ancient mariners having battled a North Sea squall. Still, old Frederic Bennett had had many a soaking on his runs, so it would have been wrong for Julian not to have at least had one and, anyway, it was nothing that a hot bath and a stiff drink were unable to cure.

The following day, arriving at Southsea in still more sunshine, although accompanied with a cool sea breeze, there this time to greet Julian were the grandson and great-grandson of his grandfather's mechanic who had been with him in 1953. Back then, as recorded in the Veteran Car Club's archive: *"On the outward journey to Southsea, the rear offside mudguard stay broke away, but was temporarily secured by Mr Bennett's mechanic, Mr Henocq, running alongside the car – despite his seventy years, he described this feat as 'normal'"*. As though nothing had changed during the intervening years, the illustrious Mr Heocq's grandson and great-grandson produced a couple of monkey wrenches – such crudities not being considered an essential part of the tool kit – and helped tighten a leaking joint on the old car's cooling system.

Once the day's formalities were over and having commiserated at the dislodging on the way down of the right-hand headlight – retrieved thankfully – the two of them gave 530 a stately motorcycle escort out of town. This left Julian to face some of the Run's fastest, almost motorway stretches of road. What an extraordinary sight: two heads & shoulders, Julian's and his navigator's, at times towering above the other cars and, at others, swamped and seemingly overrun by the enormous lorries as they swept past plying their goods between London and the south coast. Happily, car and occupants survived the ordeal, arriving back, exhausted, just before dark.

As the days progressed, we became more and more disbelieving that 530 and crew would make it to the end. Their average speed, due almost entirely to London traffic, was down to barely 14mph as against over twenty in 1953 and not far short of twenty in 1903. Julian, therefore, was spending close on ten hours a day behind the wheel of a machine whose driving stress is many times that of a modern car. Moreover, every extra hour on the road meant one less for the necessary daily preparations and one less for resting up. It was beginning to tell.

On the Wednesday, we headed off for Bexhill, the birthplace of British motor racing. There to meet us on the outskirts, chauffeured in none other than General Patton's WW2 Rolls-Royce, were both the Mayor and deputy. From there, we were convoyed regally into the centre of the town. Whereupon, as if from nowhere, we were joined by a cavalcade of multi-vintaged cars, at its head an antique steam car belching its excesses into the dry autumn air.

As we drew onto the seashore's Delawarr Parade – the very road where those early racers had competed – a band struck up, at which a barbeque, complete with fatted calf, was fired up too. Nearby, to our amazement, filled with an array of motor racing memorabilia and photographs, sat a sprawling marquee with guests milling and enquirers enquiring: and all just for us. How awful if 530 had broken down on this of all days – with or without an emergency transporter to carry Julian into town. For sure too, the Roadster's presence would only have added confusion to the situation and over-loaded some already overstretched brains.

This time to welcome Julian was the grandson of that long-time friend of Frederic Bennett and most famous of early motor racers, S F Edge. S F's wife had welcomed 'Frederic I' in 1953 and now S F's grandson presented Frederic III with a commemorative cup in appreciation of the Bennett's continuing links with Bexhill. With speeches and photo-shoots over and, capping an already astounding welcome, we, the guests of honour, were taken off and treated to a foursquare meal in a restaurant nearby.

What could anyone say to such hospitality, such generosity? Not a lot: other than a string of over-profusive thank-yous and a feeling that we would at some time want to return. Even before we could all gather together and head back, the band struck up again, the crowd re-grouped and all and everyone wished us well for the remainder of the Run. Then, as so often on both outbound and return journeys, we called and were called by media and friends alike to confer on the Run. Apart from 530's clutch having begun to slip and adding a rear mudguard to the score of accumulated losses – another non-essential and safely retrieved – that was a very satisfactory day.

The following morning, we staggered out of bed and made for Winchester, with its old-world charm and natural beauty, the only inland end-town of the Run. The meeting point, instead as with the others being on the seashore, was in the town centre, beneath King Alfred's statue in amongst the bustle of every-day shoppers and late-season tourists. What a commotion we caused: holding up traffic, diverting buses, blocking coaches and generally clogging the pavements and walkways.

A quick photo-shoot, with King Alfred's statue in the background to match that of Frederic I's arrival in the town fifty years earlier, was followed by an excellent lunch in the oldest mayoral residence in the country. Friends, relatives, enthusiasts and onlookers had all gathered to join in with the obvious pleasure that only one day remained.

Part of the tail lamp joined the 'fall off' tally that day, which, sadly, disappeared into the undergrowth. More worrying, the slipping clutch, badly contaminated by the earlier over-oiling, was getting worse; and 530 was beginning to slow. Then, no doubt for a bit of diversification, 530 ran out of fuel. The BEN vehicle entered the fray once more with jerry can and funnel. Thus the team arrived back rather later than we cared: tiredness all around setting in still further.

Apart from the clutch, which Julian feared might yet give out, the odd wheel from 1903 had become distinctly wobbly, and a couple of others, despite their nightly soaking with wet towels to help the wooden spokes expand, were beginning to do the same. There was concern also for the antique ignition system, as there was for a rear wheel bearing that was considerably looser than recommended. On the other hand, the carburettor, with Mr Single Cylinder's donated parts, was still performing superbly.

So, having at first been concerned at the possible embarrassment of an early failure, now, having achieved so much, we all, especially Julian, feared failing at the last. We knew just how he felt; just as I had felt when seven-eights through completing the Roadster – that old adage of "a miss is as good as a mile". In truth, we were all far more exhausted than we cared to admit: the support team from the constant involvement both in the daily runs and the daily organisation, and Julian due to all the driving.

On the other hand, the tiredness of Julian's navigator, an old and trusted friend and calming influence for Julian, was of a different form. Each evening, he would excuse himself and, while heading for his car, make repeated references to, "his very busy night-time schedule". Into this after-hours life, we decided not to delve too deeply, especially as he always arrived well on time each morning.

The last day's run down to Brighton, by far the shortest, is helped by the parallel motorway running almost to the coast. This considerably reduces the traffic on the old roads we were set to use but, with slipping clutch, wobbly wheels and questionable ignition, 530's speed had been reducing by the hour. We were up and about, bleary-eyed, well before breakfast; and with those welcome cloudless skies in evidence yet again.

Starting a full hour early, and nursing the clutch, Julian and his nocturnal navigator, trailed by that day's follow-up vehicle, arrived only a little late on the seafront, at the same point where the London to Brighton meets. By now, Julian and the aged 530 had completed over a thousand miles, giving the feeling to many that the challenge was over. Not so, the 1903 rules are quite clear: an entrant vehicle must, on each day of the run, return to Crystal Palace under its own power, and that included the last day to Brighton and back too.

Not withstanding this, an air of celebration prevailed. Relatives and friends and Veteran Car Club members and dignitaries, spilling out in all directions across the promenade with Brighton Pier stretching clear out behind, greeted the heroes as they arrived. The Mayor was there too, as was BBC Television and news reporters. After television interviews, photo-shoots and journalistic dialogue, the finder-owner of GM's dossier covering the 1953 Run presented it to Julian as a worthy Bennett keepsake. The BBC was then given a quick once around the seafront, after which the convoy headed north again: relatives, friends and Veteran Car Club cheering them on once more.

Mile-by-mile they headed ever closer to the finish, Julian worrying, as did we all, whether the final hill, up which they had only just managed to climb the previous day, would be the final straw.

Arriving at the bottom of the incline, Julian gripped the steering ever tighter, and prayed. Steadily, in amongst the stop-start London traffic, chug chug chug, 530 climbed inexorably upwards. At each corner, at each intersection or traffic-light, the two of them, driver and navigator, perched on high, remained ever tense; and, just like in the Middle East when two of us had ploughed through those desert dunes with that old Oldsmobile, not a word was spoken.

On they battled, ever upwards to the summit of London's highest point. Someone or something was on their side. On that sunny early-autumn afternoon, they came over the brow to reach the final straight. Mightily relieved, and spot on schedule, a victorious trio, driver, navigator and car, drove through the gates of Queens Hotel.

There to greet them with smiles and cheers all round were family and friends, representatives of the clubs and others who had gathered. There also, looking down from on high, visible in the hotel entrance at the top of those dreaded steps, was the Royal Baby Cadillac, a perfect backdrop to a truly Bennett affair. There was no mayoral reception or official welcome on this occasion. Without exception, we had all felt that to arrange for such would have tempted fate one too far.

That said, there and then, the Veteran Car Club observer confirmed the Run's official success. Cameras clicked, praise abounded and champagne appeared as if from nowhere. We grandsons of the Crewe engineers then raised a glass to each other – as no doubt did the grandfathers, relaxing comfortably somewhere on high.

Recorded for posterity in the lines of a literary output by another of the Veteran Car Club's observers: *"Of such stuff are dreams made"*.

Deservedly – or at least so we considered – we patted ourselves on the back and continued the celebrations. Eventually, we packed up and headed our separate ways: 530 trailered back to the National Motor Museum and the Roadster, embarrassingly, perched high on the back of an RAC transporter.

For all that, we were heading home knowing that a very special milestone had been achieved: man & machine – or, more correctly, family & machine – had successfully notched up another fifty years.

18. Resting Up

As long ago as December 1900, the 'Self-propelled Traffic Association' reported: *"England will be benefited, not – as some think – rendered unfit to live in, by the habitual use of an invention which, by circulating wealth and promoting activity in stagnant places, by revealing to men the beauties of their native land, takes it place with its two great predecessors as a factor in the welfare of the community at large."* and so it went on, expounding the wonders of a coming age.

A century later, on our week of southern travels, we discovered just that. The better the main through routes, regardless of the state of the secondary, more local roads, the greater the overall affluence of an area. Wherever a motorway has been added, the secondary roads for some distance around are far more peaceful and the countryside less spoilt. Furthermore, the representative of BEN, who accompanied us all the way, observed that far from detrimentally scarring the landscape, these man-made creations, snaking into the middle distance, are more a thing of inspiration, and perfectly in keeping with the rolling greenery to each side.

That prediction had certainly come true but nobody would have thought back then that an obscure entrant in the 1903 Trial would, a hundred years later, on some of those roads achieve its fourth 1,000-mile success. BEN, the motor trades charity, were as delighted with the money raised from the Run as they were with all the publicity. Reported in newspapers all along the south coast, once and mostly twice in each location, as well as in motoring magazines and other national publications, had to be a major plus. Even the Roadster, despite its ultimate inactivity, had an occasional mention too.

On top of this, to have featured in three separate TV News reports was an unexpected bonus; and, if not for the sudden arrival on the last day at Heathrow Airport of Mathew Scott, the kidnap victim recently escaped from Columbian rebels, Julian would have been on London Evening News and likely National News too – just as his grandfather had been. However, such bravery in the Amazon was considered more than worthy an adversary for having our TV crew pulled at the last moment.

When recounting this some months later to Algi, that ever-questioning pin-stripe suited banker, a cousin of his with him declared: "Oh yes, Mathew Scott, I remember the incident well... as the Foreign Office representative on call at the time, I accompanied him back to London on the plane. In fact, I even had to say a few words to the BBC... I suppose into that very same camera and crew!" Yet another coincidence to add to the ever-growing string.

Further afield, congratulations on Julian's success came from none other than the committed enthusiast and then Chairman of GM USA, Bob Lutz. His short message ended with the simple but meaningful words: "Splendid job, kudos to all."

Despite all this eulogy from on high, when the Club's home video of the event came out, who, of all those involved, was to receive star billing? One of us hard-working men perhaps, or even the rightfully-deserving Julian? No, yet again, the single-handed *Back-up* had moved solidly *up front*, heading the list for her outstanding organisation at the Queens Hotel.

Still, without her initial "what a good idea" at my light-hearted suggestion of "we'll have to make one", such a string of events would never have been set in motion and the centennial challenge would not have taken place. That said, what if the re-run had ended in embarrassing failure and best never to have taken place at all? The answer to that must surely be the same as the Scandinavian truck driver's answer to the state of the weather on the eve of the event: "But it dose-ent happen, so vhy vorry!"

What then of the criticism by the Veteran Car Club observer on day one of the lack of proper preparation? As Frederic Bennett had always boasted that 'Old Dutch', as he called 530, never needed any particular preparation for its 1,000-miles – roadworthiness alone was good enough – who were we to change that now? Anyway, at the Veteran Car Club's Annual General Meeting in the hallowed confines of the RAC Club, Julian, along with being given as promised a signed authentication certificate to match that produced in 1953, was showered with praise and presented with the trophy for that year's outstanding achievement.

Extraordinary as it now began to seem, Julian had, with minimal preparation, managed to cover those twenty London to Brighton Runs in nine short days after all. Eight on the daily runs and the ninth, slotted between day two and day three, at the special 'rest day' show in Crystal Palace Park.

What of the Show? Well, in near mid-summer weather, a splendid collection of the likes of Genevieve, alongside rakish 30s and 40s cars, together with chromiumed 50s, 60s and 70s blending with the more subdued 80's, 90s and millennias, were all there. The US Club's delegates from the south and the north, the ones who had originally instigated the grand plan, were all there too; but the cow-horned classic from Texas, sadly, was not. The array posed gracefully in the park on the neatly kept undulating lawns, elegantly backed with greens and browns of a nearing autumn. There was music, there were speeches and there was a Grand Parade ranging through the decades, including, of course, the Maharajah and his magnificent V16.

"What a beautiful car," someone would observe, to which the 'Mahah' would reply: "Yes, it's a 1931 Dual Cowl Phaeton made for the Maharajah of Tikari, and the only one of its type." Whereupon, still expounding the qualities of his elegant two-and-three-quarter ton car, he would suddenly ask: "Who would like a ride?" At which a whole *four* could clamber in, and off they would set around the park. Then again, and much to the horror of his insurers, he might just as suddenly pull over and declare: "Go on, take the wheel, you drive!" If brave you be, take the wheel you did; and much pleasure derived too. Tirelessly, continuously, hour after hour, he gave his all, literally, to one and all.

On top of that, having the likes of Sir Stirling Moss and other celebrities attend, what more could one ask? They too seemed to enjoy themselves. Stirling was certainly sporting a smile when the show organiser, open armed and for all to hear, greeted him with a loud, "Stirling, my boyhood hero... I can't believe it's really you!" to which he gave Stirling a great hug. Our celebrated guest still had a broad smile when trying his hand behind the wheel of the Maha's pride and joy, to say nothing of his testing one or two other lavish machines on the remains of the circuit he remem-bered so well from earlier years.

What then, in the end, did he make of the Roadster? Well, he certainly wanted to know all about it. He sat inside to get a good feel and to have a look along that truck-like bonnet, a contented smile emanating from in there too. Then, at the end of the day, having seen all the cars and driven several, Stirling declared that the latest low-slung 160-mph STS Seville and the Roadster, jointly, were his choice. What, though, did he think of how the Roadster drove? Well that was the pity: he never did because he never could. I had put pay to that the day before with my idiotic argument with the concrete slab.

Still, for Sir Stirling Moss to have complimented the Roadster the way he did was more than reward enough. Those earlier assessments by others at Goodwood were already far more than any would-be carmakers could reasonably have expected. Anyway, Lady Moss had said "no" to our intended antics; so, better to have complied than to have defied. Stirling, having been presented with a commemorative cut-glass decanter, was duly ferried back to his now repaired car without a spare; and so ended for him what he kindly wrote and described as "a quite exceptional day".

There, that day too, to continue the link begun more than a century earlier, was the third grandson of the three Crewe engineers. He and I reminisced over that other fine car that we had both used and abused: the Chicken Manure Special. It would, we concluded, have loved to have joined in the day. Yet, as we both knew, as with that old Buick at university, with the likes of us having been involved, she had simply died: her time had come.

Then there is that other question: "What's the Roadster called?" For sure, while undergoing its massive reconstruction, all sorts of names, few of which could be repeated here. On the other hand, its project name, being the simple addition of our old company's name, Courier Products, was the Courier-Cadillac, often as not shortened to 'Courillac' or even 'Couriadillac'. Alternatively, in its home town, after its rise to fame, the one-off local creation has long since been known as 'The Haverhill Car' and, as such, used to promote the town's ever-expanding manufacturing expertise.

If it had to have a name, what then? Well, the name 'Cad's Car', as shouted one day at Silverstone from behind the wheel of one those elegant round-bonnet racers of yesteryear – the driver not aware of its parentage – was a name that nearly stuck: but not quite. Even the 'Coincidence Car', so obvious a tag, never stood much of a chance. It has also variously been known as the 'Noddy Car' – as it only fits two

– and, rather rudely by the owner of an elderly Morris Minor, as the 'Kit Car', to which we always reply with, "And how's the Dinky Toy?"

There was the other possibility, when two great nieces over from America aged three and five wanted a ride in what they referred to as 'great uncle's Chitty'. Having strapped them securely into the passenger seat side by side, off we set. After a silent several hundred yards, I announced that we would attempt 'take off'. On engaging Bill's better breathing, producing its deep-throated rumble from beneath, the little eyes lit up. After a second or two, I floored the accelerator, surging forward with that thunderous roar. Then, while apparently propelled by some magic after-burner, I swayed back and forth and prompted a "come on, come on... up we go!"

The wide-eyed reaction from two little faces beside me was glorious to perceive in itself. What I had not counted on, though, was the low flying pigeon that, at my very suggestion of being airborne, flew past the passenger window. Now, nothing will persuade the younger of the two that great-uncle's 'Chitty' had not flown, and the elder is still not wholly convinced either way.

For all that, and despite the many Professor Potts antics during its making, 'Chitty' never stuck either. Even with its fixed roof, and therefore not truly a Roadster, our one-off creation is just called the Seville Roadster, or the Roadster for short; and, despite all the coincidences and everything else, that is that.

As for those links and coincidences: how unlikely they were, and each so crucial to the next. For all that, were we ever in the least bit sensible in starting the project, thereby setting the string in motion? On that score, a statement voiced very early on by an American always leaps to mind: "Only a crazy bunch of Englishmen could have done that to one of our best cars!" Maybe so: but, since that time, we crazy Englishmen have not only managed to unearth some hitherto unrealised motoring history, re-discovered family members and old friends – to say nothing of new friends made – but we have had all the enjoyment of so doing. Finally, we helped create an endurance yardstick in the realms of modern motoring history that none had foreseen.

So, with the Roadster now safely back on the road with the exhaust suitably repaired by the welder of the impossible, perhaps a more relaxed retirement has been earned, both for car and keeper alike.

Young Gavin's view, on seeing the result of 530's rant at the Roadster's tail, was simple: "Well Boss, you're both getting older... you should take it easy now!"

When I pointed out that the cause of the Roadster's affliction is some three-quarters of a century older than the Roadster and very considerably older than me, he merely quipped: "Ah, but that's a real car, that's different!"

I suppose such a rebuke must mean that Gavin, despite his enduring input to the Roadster, considers one-off specials to be a peculiarity that do not properly equate to his trade. That said, the now not-so-young Professor of Bodies has always had a soft spot for a car that, by all our admissions, "gave us much brain ache" and "taught us a thing or two".

Apart from some gentle summer use, attendance at car shows and an occasional sprint on the track, what of the Roadster's future then? Will it the sink back into oblivion or are a string of new excitements waiting round the corner? Julian, when asked at the end of the run, just as his grandfather had been fifty years earlier, whether he would be doing it again in fifty years time replied: "When deciding whether or not to take on the 2003 challenge, one of my sons said 'Dad, if *you* don't do it in 2003, how can *we* do it in 2053?' So, I hope at least to be there to cheer them on."

If that be the case, will the Roadster be there too – hopefully, with 530 being a little kinder to its finder in half a century's time? Also, will others of another generation of those involved in 2003 be involved then as well? Of that, only the future can tell.

In the end, for all the coincidences and hows and whys, there can still only be one conclusion to the Roadster's singular being. For one, we were undoubtedly more than a trifle barmy ever to have started the project and, for another, we were more than mildly optimistic in thinking that our limited-edition motorcar, a product of the late eighties boom and a casualty of the early nineties recession, should end up as any more than a very limited edition – of *one*.

End

Epilogue

Having started the book at the beginning of 1993, GM Public Relations were contacted that November and in early 1994 'Cadillac Voice' carried the article that lead to so much else. By the time 'so much else' had happened, old Jaws had clocked up over 300,000 miles, the Roadster nearly 40,000 and the final chapters were eventually completed a full decade on.

Now, seventeen years after the arrival of the inspirational postcard, Jack has sold his business, Bruce has long since returned from Australia to continue his 'creating' and Des has retired and handed over to the next generation, who in turn have sold the business on. Frank is as involved as ever with his farming and classic cars, and Bill continues his dedication to all things Morgan. Tom has left the motor trade for general industry, Alan still has his electrical concern and Gavin is one of the top independent coachbuilders in the country.

A further unexpected discovery – also in part turned up by the Roadster – shows a friendly ongoing Trans-Atlantic link between GM America and Rolls-Royce in Crewe. In the archives of the Rolls-Royce Enthusiasts Club is evidence that the two companies co-operated right through from the late nineteen-twenties into the nineteen-sixties and beyond.

The present-day descendants of those characters of a century earlier, Julian Bennett, Ivor Faulconer and William Leland, have no doubt that Frederic Bennett, Robert Faulconer and Henry Leland would have welcomed such an ongoing Anglo-American relationship. Furthermore, in the Bennett archives was the surprise discovery that not only did my maternal grandfather and Fred Bennett study engineering together at Crewe but they also started their working life in the same London company.

So, such is truth as against fiction; and for all those around in 2053, keep an eye on events at Crystal Palace Park from 18th to 25th September that year.

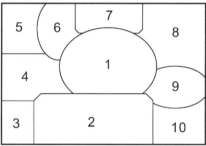

1. The FA Cup 'photo shoot' at the town exhibition.
2. Partly built with insets of several key participants.
3. Promoting Haverhill's manufacturing expertise.
4. The 'C M' Special as last seen by the editor in Africa.
5. Sir Stirling Moss back in the driving seat fifty years later.
6. Uncle Ruddy and nephew 'on the box' circa 1910.
7. The front of the auctioneer's 'inspirational' postcard.
8. Success on the first day of the Centennial Challenge.
9. The Leland & Faulconer factory in Detroit circa 1900.
10. Ready for competition in Crystal Palace Park.